Information Literacy

Essential Skills for the Information Seekers in the Digital Age

Information Literacy

Essential Skills for the Information Seekers in the Digital Age

DR. RAJEEV MISHRA

Delta Book World

New Delhi-110002

First Published in 2018
ISBN 978-93-85719-11-0

Published by
Delta Book World
G-4, Prahlad House
4832/24, Ansari Road
New Delhi - 110 002 (India)
Tel.: 011-4707 2321
E-mail: deltabookworld@gmail.com

Laser Typesetting by : Tamalika Computers, Delhi

PRINTED IN INDIA

Dedicated to

My Parents, my wife and lovely daugher

for their constant support and encouragement

Acknowledgement

First I would like to express my endless gratitude to God, the Almighty, the most generous, who provided me with all the necessary strength and guidance for the timely completion of this volume without whose blessings nothing could be done.

It gives me immense pleasure to express my heartfelt thanks to all those who helped me directly and indirectly in the successful completion of the volume.

Now I would like to express my deep sense of gratitude and sincere thanks to my teacher Prof. (Dr.) M.T.M. Khan, Dean, School of Library and Information Science, Galgotias University, Greater Noida, for his support and constant advice, constructive criticism and guidance which helped me to understand the theoretical and practical aspects of the work.

I am thankful to the distinguished Librarians, Dr. Akhtar Parvez, Librarian IIM, Indore, Dr. M.K. Singh, Deputy Librarian, IIM Lucknow, Dr. Neeraj Chaurasia, Deputy Librarian, IIT Delhi, Mr. Ram Naresh Indoria, Sr. Lib. & Information Assistant, IIT Roorkee, Dr. Ashok Kumar Upadhyaya, BML Munjal University, Gurugram and Shri Ranjan Tandon for their moral support, constant persuasion and guidance during my research work.

I am also thankful to Dr. R.K. Sharma, Librarian, United Nations Information Centre, Dr. S. Majumdar, Chief Librarian, and other authorities of India International Centre who always encouraged me and smoothened the path for this endeavour.

I would like to thanks the library staff of India International Centre for providing necessary help.

During the completion of this work, I could not perform my basic responsibilities towards my family members. I must extend my sincere heart-felt thanks and appreciation to my parents, my wife and my lovely daughter. They always gave me love, affection and encouragement to achieve this goal.

(Rajeev Mishra)

Preface

We live in an information intensive world. Every human being seeks and uses information to meet all the fundamental requirements of life. Information literacy is essential for individuals to achieve their personal, social and educational goals. It is a key factor in producing effective lifelong learners and creating knowledge-based societies. The development of such skills takes place throughout a citizen's life especially during the educational years when librarians and experts in information management play major roles in facilitating information literacy. However, information literacy needs to be considered in education. The present volume is the revised version of my thesis entitled "Information Literacy among users of select IIT and IIM Libraries: A Comparative study" from Galgotias University, Greater Noida.

This volume is an attempt for introduce the science, technology and management-related information available to students, research scholars and faculty members in a more reliable form. The study shows that an information literacy programme is inevitable and necessary for students, research scholars and faculty members to make them more information literate. Information literacy instructions and training programmes need to be organized on a regular basis owing to the rapid growth of electronic and web-based information resources.

Management and technology library professionals should do efforts to develop complete training programme or information literacy course not only for PG students and research scholars but for faculty members and UG students also, so that the existing gap between the capabilities and skills of the students and faculty can be improved. The library and information science professionals and teachers can do a lot to achieve this goal. The volume is structured in the following chapters:

Chapter 1 presents an overview and nature of research study undertaken and also provides a comprehensive explanation of information literacy. The chapter begins with information literacy, its evolution, different concepts, definition, objectives, scope and significance, and need and limitations of the study.

Chapter 2 discusses the exploration of the methodological framework of the study.

Chapter 3 includes the process and outcome of an exploratory survey done in select IIT and IIM libraries. This chapter represents the analysis and interpretation of data collected through various tools. The researcher interacted with almost all the librarians and users of the libraries and assisted them in filling the questionnaires. A personal visit to the libraries helped the researcher to gather more information and see the actual services provided by them.

The collected data has been organized and tabulated by simple statistical methods. The purpose of analysis is to shape data to intelligible forms, that the relation of research problems can be studied and tested.

Chapter 4 discusses the major findings, which have been drawn on the basis of data collected from the four institutes under the study. Tenability of the hypotheses is checked with the help of independent t-test as a statistical tool and suggestions are provided to improve the information literacy skills in research scholars and PG students in the IIT and IIM libraries. At the end some recommendation and possible areas for further research also have been mentioned in this chapter.

(Rajeev Mishra)

Contents

List of Tables

List of Figures

17. Hindrances Encountered by respondents in Information Literacy Programmes
18. Satisfaction level of the Respondents
19. Need of Training

List of Abbreviations

AASL	American Association of School Librarians
ACRL	American College of Research Libraries
ACRL	Association of College and Research Libraries
ALA	American Library Association
ANZIIL	Australian and New Zealand Institute for Information Literacy
CD-ROM	Compact Disk-Read Only Memory
CILIP	Chartered Institute of Library and Information Professionals
CLA	Canadian Library Association
EnIL	European Network for Information Literacy
IFLA	International Federation of Library Association and Institutions
IIMI	Indian Institute of Management Indore
IIML	Indian Institute of Management Lucknow
IITD	Indian Institute of Technology Delhi
IITR	Indian Institute of Technology Roorkee
IL	Information Literacy
ILIG	Information Literacy Interest Group
ILP	Information Literacy Programme

IT	Information Technology
OPAC	Online Public Access Catalogue
PG	Post Graduate
RS	Research Scholar
SCONUL	Society of College & New University Libraries
UNESCO	United Nations Educational, Scientific & Cultural Organisation
WWW	World Wide Web

1

Introduction

The aim of this chapter is to present an overview and nature of research study undertaken for the users. The objective of the chapter is to provide a comprehensive explanation of information literacy. The chapter begins with information literacy, its evolution, various concepts, definitions, objectives, scope, significance, need and limitations of the study.

1.0 INTRODUCTION

We live in an information intensive world. Information has come to occupy a predominant position in the decision-making process. It is the need of the hour for all, to decipher the environment and make our way through the world. Economic, political, technological, military and social power of information is easily noticeable. It is an important resource for overall development and is the most valuable possession any society has. Knowledge is culture, passed on from generation to generation (Khairah, 2005).

It is easier for individual to access information at any place, time and about anything. The reason being the recent developments in information communication technologies and globalization of information. (Karisiddappa,2014)

The information social structure is witness to a vast and ever increasing variety of information, embodied in myriad formats and a distinct advancement of technology. To lead a successful life, it is a prerequisite for students to be information competent. Thus, it is a prerogative of educational institutions to help students develop this competency and become well-informed citizens of a society established on platforms of information and technology.

Over the past few years, information literacy skills form an integral part of a graduate's attributes. A gradual shift in focus from content to critical thinking and lifelong learning has been noticed. It is a move from teacher-centred teaching to student-centred learning. In this shift, importance of information literacy is increasingly recognized within academic and non-academic communities.

1.1 EVOLUTION OF INFORMATION LITERACY

Zurkowski first used the term 'Information Literacy' in 1974. Ever since its coinage, the idea has been evolving and has expanded beyond the field of Library Science. This growth has been noticed not only in United States but even in other countries throughout the world. The advent of "information explosion" has become a source of concern for the Librarians. The idea of Information Literacy is to enable people to be successful users of information. This is the answer to the continuous expansion of information and its evolution. In other words, Information explosion which was the point of worry for the librarians could be solved with information literacy. 'Those from fields outside Library Science have also acknowledged the effects of the exponential growth of information' (Eisenberg, 2004). It is important to first know the origin and exact meaning of the term 'Information Literacy' before understanding about the concept. The word Information descended from a Latin word '*Informare*', a verb. It later evolved into use as noun 'Information', meaning concept or idea. 'Literate' comes from the Latin term '*Literatus*' which means learned or lettered.

1.2 INFORMATION LITERACY

Information Literate are individuals those who are empowered to classify and categorize information. They have the understanding to evaluate, locate and use the adequate information which guides them toward the correct source of reliable information. It is to know details and source of information itself. Information literacy is important for individuals to reach their desired goal in any field. It is pivotal factor in creating individuals who are effective learners and knowledge based societies.

The development of such skills takes place throughout a citizen's life especially during the educational years whence librarians and experts in information management play major roles in facilitating information literacy.

Information literacy needs to be considered not only in relation to education but also in the broader context of work, civil society, health and well-being (Garner, 2003). Information Literacy means to aid a person realizing the need for information. Individuals who are Information Literate strategize their priorities like health, environment, education and work and gain appropriation information. Therefore, it helps them to make critical decisions about their lives. Just like taking informed choice and responsibility regarding health and education. Apart from this, there are many ways to understand this complex yet necessary term. Various experts have their own views and research about the same.

It is also important for students to be made information literate. The need to be Information Literate is essential as each generation is increasingly involved with technology. As the technology immensely contributes to information overload, the necessary is lost in abundance. Students must be made aware of various print and electronic resources which include networked databases, the World Wide Web and traditional print resources. They should be able to protect themselves against false information by evaluating the sources. They must also be able to make proper decision on selection of appropriate information according to their needs. Each institution must develop elective use of learning resources. This to be done through a concrete plan which helps students inculcates information literacy. It is essential to have an active and continuing programme of library orientation. To add, the programme must have instruction in accessing information developed collaboratively, supported actively by faculty, librarians, academicians and other providers. (Konnur, 2011)

Developing a common information literacy education programme for the library has many advantages. A formalized user education programme ensures better quality in procedures regarding collaboration with the faculty. It informs all higher education partners about the kind of information literacy, teaching and supervision the library supports. A formal programme further shows the faculty how the library has interpreted and integrated the general visions and pedagogical goals of the institution in its user education.

Within the library, a potential danger when developing a formalized common user education programme is that library staff might consider it too rigid in its framework. They might feel that the programme has been imposed on them by the library management, and that it is difficult to interpret, modify, or adapt to their ever changing teaching reality. It is thus of paramount importance that the library management involves their teaching library staff in (1) the process of laying the pedagogical foundations of the library user education, and (2) the process of designing a common information literacy programme. Involving library staff in the education planning process will be beneficial for the institution and their professionals (Torras and Setre, 2009).

1.3 DIMENSIONS OF INFORMATION LITERACY

Information Literacy cannot be explained completely in words given its comprehensive nature and ever evolving process of educating. It can be summarized through its wide range of fields which are mentioned below.

Media Literacy: In order to communicate effectively, the images must be created and proposed with the collective understanding in a variety of media. This skill in an individual is known as Media Literacy.

Network Literacy: As the name suggests, it is the ability to network (manage, connect and assess) after evaluating information from various sources and obtain in a correct way.

Web Literacy: It comes under the bracket of information literacy which requires the skill to reach, create or pass information through the World Wide Web (WWW).

Digital Literacy: The aptitude required to use (assess, collect, organize, evaluate) digital resources and service to maximize collection of coherent information.

Scientific Literacy: Scientific literacy is the knowledge of concepts and processes that are required for personal decision making, involvement in civic or cultural affairs and economic productivity.

Virtual Literacy: Virtual literacy is the ability to understand and use images. This includes thinking, learning, and expressing oneself in terms of images. Photographs, cartoons, line drawings, diagrams, concepts, maps, and other visual representations are all important in visual literacy.

Visual Literacy: Visual literacy is the ability to understand and use images.

Critical Literacy: It is the ability to critically evaluate the cost of information technology in its complete and true demeanor. It would include it intellectual, social strengths and benefits.

The other dimensions related to information literacy are, (i) Library Orientations (ii) Bibliographic Instruction (iii) User Education, and (iv) Training on Information Skills. While, the

Figure 1:
Schematic View of Dimensions of Information Literacy (Mishra, R.N., 2010)

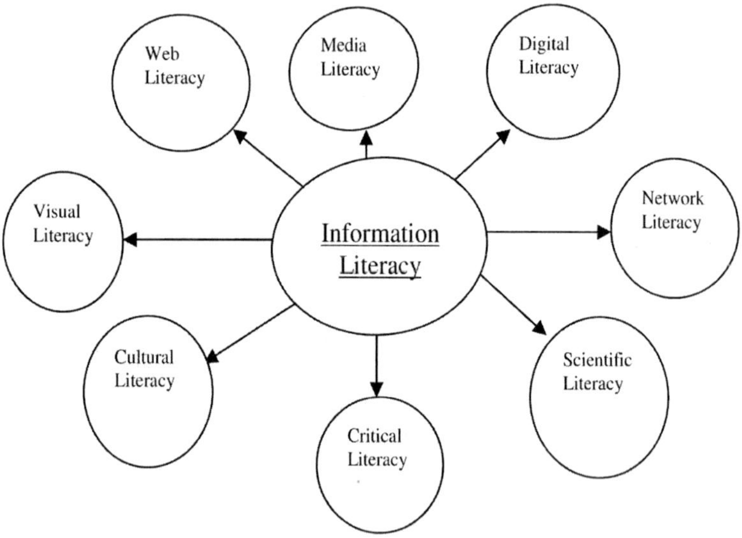

library orientation concentrates on using a library and its sections including location of resources, bibliographic instruction emphasizes the location of documents in the library. The user education is related with the mechanics involved for using particular resources. Training on information skills is related with the phenomena associated with the use of technology to retrieve information in the library. (Mishra, R. N., 2010).

1.4 DIFFERENT CONCEPTS OF INFORMATION LITERACY

Variety of concepts of information literacy have been brought up and changed over time. These information skills are focused on programmes such as Information Fluency, User Education, Library Instruction, Bibliographic Instruction, Information Competencies, Information Skills, User Training and User Orientation.

Library Orientation: This term refers to efficiently using the library and this branching sections including the location of the resources.

Bibliographic Instruction: This presses on the location of the documents within the library. The user is trained on searching and retrieving information.

User Education: This involves the understanding to use the resources strategically for information.

Training on Information Skills: Using technology to extract information in the library requires training on Information skills.

Information Competencies: The compact aim of information literacy is known as Information Competencies.

Information Skills: The skills required to get the information is known as Information Skills.

1.5 NEED AND IMPORTANCE OF INFORMATION LITERACY

Information technology has brought about radical changes in the field related to information namely Information acquisition, Information organization, Information management and dissemination of information. With the introduction of different tools to access information, it has been easier to adapt to the changing situation.

On the other hand, the users are unable to access through ever evolving technology. The infinite probability of different version information and ever expanding quantity of the same poses a major threat to the society. The identification of rapid change in technology in addition to proliferation of information sources has commenced the shift of specifications from library to information literacy.

The individuals who wish to access correct information are faced with multitudes of information due to which constraints them in making major choices. The design of digital environment does not subdue complexities rather encourages it. As the complexities increase, the individual is faced with unverified information which further confuses them. In the end, this does not bring solution but question about authenticity, validity and reliability.

Moreover, this information is presented through different medias such as graphical, acoustic, visual, textual etc. These present new challenges in understanding and filtering the information for a user. (Mishra, R. N., 2010).

Nowadays, libraries contain both traditional and ICT based services. All the services and resources bought by the libraries aid in acquiring, organizing, circulating and disseminating huge information sources.

Also, the ICT as a resource as become a ground that provides the ability to create and provide information. Additionally, the users too, find it useful for their research and development activities. Newage technology wherein information is able in form of e-journals, e-books, CD-ROMs etc are yet to be brought to the notice of users. Through a brief orientation, the users will be able to utilize the information.

Also, they need to be aware of the role of e-portals, information gateways and need special skills to be developed for using such facilities with maximum benefit (Bhatt, R. K., 2011).

Lastly, the users are to be aware of the role of e-portals, information gateways. Specific skills are to be nurtured in the user to use such facilities to their maximum.

It is a part of our ethics as information literacy educators that we teach ourselves and to the community what the inter-relation of global learning and information literacy are made off. It is also to be brought to notice what we as educators contribute to this.

Ideas about global learning have been exchanged a few times on our campuses. On a meta level, it can be considered that we have not engaged to our full capabilities in these campus wide conversations. This also includes conversations regarding one's role as educator within the global learning context.

It time to realize that we must become active part of this conversation. We must consider what we contribute to this and use our leadership as the information literacy experts on campus. This calls for us to be a part of an age where one of the fundamental attributes of the world is digital globalized information society. Today, in this day and age, inability to access information or use information for any reason is a substantive disadvantage.

Today, as manual library catalogues have become computerized, it has become difficult to locate the required information. The retrieval of information in a computerized system takes less time compared to the manual system, but the decision-making has become a more complex process. A working knowledge of computers is a must to operate databases. The users also need to evaluate the database best suited to their information needs. The users need to be aware of the different search engines to search for information available on the Internet. They also require knowledge of different search strategies. Searching for any information on the internet retrieves many documents which require an evaluation of the retrieved information on the part of the users for relevance. Thus, a user needs to evaluate the usefulness, accuracy and relevance of the retrieved information, be it in electronic from or print form. Such skills are required for a person to be information literate.

Information literacy as a skill is very important in the current times as it helps in maximum utilization of vast information resources. It makes the user competent enough to extract relevant and exact information according to their need.(Jnanendra and Joshi, 2006)

1.6 INFORMATION LITERACY MODELS

Different models have been developed and propagated by authors, theorists and academicians.

Information Search Process (Kuhlthau, C. C., 1993)

The Information Search process model based on a constructive approach was developed by Kuhlthau. The model has seven stages which includes initiation, selection prefocus exploration, formulation, collection, presentation and assessment. This model demonstrates users' approach to the research process and how users' confidence increases.

In 1999, the SCONUL Advisory committee on Information Literacy came up with model consisting of seven level of competence called the Seven Pillars of Information Literacy. It comprised of:

a. Skill to recognize need for information
b. To know different ways the need is to be addressed
c. To make strategies for identifying information
d. Skill to access different sources and comparing the information
e. To appropriate and communicate information
f. Being able to bridge gap by existing information
g. Providing to create new knowledge

The Big Skills (Eisenberg and Berkowitz, 1990)

This is a process model developed to solve an information problem. This has six stages of information problem solving process. It is a general attribute that students apply in their information problem solving process which are identifying the task, planning to seek information, location of information, accessing it and lastly, use of information synthesis and evaluation.

Research Process Model (Stripling and Pitts, 1998)

The model is used by students as a guide through the stages of creating a research paper. It has ten steps starting from choosing a research topic and ending with the presentation of the final topic.

Pathways to Knowledge (Pappas and Tepe, 2002)

The information enquiry model by Pappas and Tepe includes pathways to knowledge and is meant to encourage students to continuously explore and reassess as they go about with their information process. The model has six steps, namely appreciation and enjoyment, pre-search, search, interpretation, communication and evaluation.

1.7 INFORMATION LITERACY STANDARDS

There are some well-known information literacy standards:

a. Information Literacy Standards for Student Learning published by the ASSL.

b. IL Standards published by IFLA.

c. ISTE's National Educational Technology Standards (NETS).

d. Information Literacy Standard for Science and Technology by ALA/ACRL/STS Task Force on Information Literacy for Science and Technology.

e. Information Literacy Standard for Student Learning by American Association of School Librarians and Association for Educational Communications and Technology in 1998.

f. Information Literacy Competency Standards for Higher Education by Association of College and Research Libraries (ACRL) in 2000. (Bhatt, 2011).

The popular and wide accepted ACRL standards includes probable outcomes under each performance indicator. It was developed keeping in mind the need to provide guidance in the development, assessment methods, instrument and strategies for measuring student's learning outcomes. This provided a basic framework for examining information literate user.

Standard One

The amount of information needed is determined by an information literate student.

Performance Indicators

a. An information literate student states the need for information efficiently.
b. An information literate student is familiar with different varieties of potential sources for information.
c. An information literate student takes into account pros and cons of acquiring the needed information.
d. An information literate student checks again the nature and extent of the required information.

Standard Two

The information literate student accesses the required information effectively and efficiently.

Performance Indicators

a. The information literate student selects the most appropriate investigative methods of information retrieval systems for accessing the needed information.
b. The information literate student constructs and implements effectively designed search strategies.
c. The information literate student retrieves information online or in person using various methods.

d. The information literate student refines the search strategy if necessary.

e. The information literate student extracts, records, and manages the information and its sources.

Standard Three

An information literate student contrasts information and its sources. They ,then, incorporate the selected information into their knowledge base.

Performance Indicators

a. An information literate student identifies and extracts crisp points from information gathered.

b. An information literate student regulates primary criteria to contrast both the information and its sources.

c. An information literate student devices ,from the existing information, constructs of new concepts.

d. An information literate student contrast the new information with knowledge that already exist. It is to be aware of the new layers added, deduced, contrasted or understand the uniqueness of information.

e. An information literate student understands the influence of the new information on an individual's value system. Further, they try to bridge the gap between the two.

f. An information literate student affirms his/her understanding of the information through a conversation with other information literate individual, subject-area experts and/or practitioners.

g. An information literate student, lastly, decides whether the existing information satisfies the need or must the query be revised.

Standard Four

An information literate individual, by themselves or in a group, has the knowledge to utilize the gathered information to satisfy the specific need.

Performance Indicators

a. To plan and create a particular product or performance, an information literate student has to apply the new and prior information which he/she possesses.

b. The development process has to be then revised by the information literate student for the product or the performance.

c. The information literate student is required to communicate the product or performance in an effective manner to others.

Standard Five

To ensure the ethical and legal use of information, it is very important for the information literate student to understand the various economic, legal and socio-economic issues that surround the access use of information.

Performance Indicators

a. Many of the ethical, legal and socio-economic issues surrounding information and information technology need to be understood by the information literate student.

b. The laws, regulations, institutional policies, and etiquettes related to the access and use of information resources are all requires to be followed by an information literate student.

c. It is essential for an information literate student to acknowledge and understand the use of information sources in communicating the product or performance (Bhatt, 2011).

The Council of Australian University Librarians (CAUL) Information Literacy Standards (CAUL, 2001)

The University of South Australia for the Council of Australian University Librarians (CAUL) initiated and conducted a National workshop from 22nd to 23rd September, 2000 wherein IL standards for higher education were produced by The Council of Australian University Librarians (CUAL) in 2001. These standards were more intuitive than the ACRL standards and they presumed different level of thinking skills based on the relational model of information literacy developed by Christine Bruce.

a. Recognizing the need for information and determining the nature and extent of the information needed is an important trait of an information literate person.

b. The information required should be accessed effectively and efficiently by the information literate.

c. Another important skill of information literate includes evaluating information and its sources critically and incorporating only selected information into their knowledge base and value system.

d. Classification, manipulation and redrafting of the information collected should also be known by the information literate person.

e. Another common skill set includes reframing or creating new knowledge by integrating prior knowledge and new understandings both as an individual or as a member of a group.

f. Understanding cultural, economical, legal and social issues surrounding the use of information and then accessing and using information ethically, legally and respectfully should be done by an information literate.

g. Lastly, needless to say that an information literate person must recognize that information literacy is required for lifelong learning and participative citizenship.

Information Literacy Standards for Teacher Education

The data education norms for educators were affirmed by the ACRL Board of Directors on May 11, 2011. The primary motivation behind the Information Literacy Standards for Teacher Education are to:

a. Guide instructor training staff and train administrators in creating data proficiency direction for potential educator instruction understudies.

b. Empower the assessment and evaluation of such direction and educational program through benchmarking results.

c. The models additionally mean to lead instructor training understudies to consider how they may incorporate data proficiency into their future educational modules, guideline, and evaluation exercises once they progress toward becoming individuals from the instructing calling.

d. The information literate teacher education characterizes and explains the requirement for data and chooses techniques and apparatuses to find that data.

e. The information literate teacher education finds and chooses data in view of its fittingness to the particular data require and the formative needs of the students.

f. The information literate teacher education student arranges and investigations the data with regards to particular data needs and the formative propriety for the gathering of people.

g. The information literate teacher education student orchestrates, procedures, and presents the data in a way that is suitable for the reason for which data is required.

h. The information literate teacher education student assesses discrete snippets of data and also the whole data looking for process.

i. The information literate teacher education student knows how to morally utilize and disperse data.

However, the gauges are utilized as a manual for evaluation, it has been discovered that utilization of these principles on the school grounds has not been outright. Or maybe pieces have been utilized as a system for exchange and parts have been embraced to mirror the need of electorates.

Cain (2002) has been reproachful of the gauges as an evaluation instrument. She asserted that evaluation instruments accept that there is recognizable confirmation or proof of what is being measured. Without a solid comprehension of what is implied by data and with manners of thinking and so forth being hard to quantify precisely, applying norms may well outcome in the estimation of existing information as opposed to advancement of learning. (Cain, 2002)

The importance of these information literacy standards for higher education lies in the that it provides frameworks for teaching information literacy as well as assessing the information literacy level of individuals (Senlson and Stillwell, 2001).

1.8 INFORMATION LITERACY: GLOBAL SCENARIO

There are many organizations and associations around the world which have taken the initiative to promote information literacy. The following are a portion of the worldwide stages from where the ideas of information literacy have picked up energy.

CILIP: The Chartered Institute of Library and Information Professionals (CILIP) has a sub group called the Information Literacy Group. The Information Literacy Group aims to provide a forum for discussion which encourages debate and allows the exchange of knowledge in all aspects of information literacy by organizing conferences and publishing the Information Literacy Journal (http://www.cilip.org.uk)

ALA: The American Library Association (ALA) is known to support the ACRL, American Association of College & Research Libraries and the AASL, the American Association of School Librarians in the creation of information literacy material. (http://www.informationliteracy.org.uk/il-orgnisations-uk/il-organisations-international/).

CLA: The Canadian Library Association additionally has an Information Literacy Interest Group. The motivation behind the ILIG is to advance information literacy proficiency guideline as a necessary library benefit, give a gathering to dialog of exercises, projects and difficulties in information literacy, add to the instruction and preparing of curators in the conveyance, advancement and assessment of information literacy programs and to fill in as a channel of correspondence on information literacy. (http://www.cla.ca)

EnIL: The European System for information literacy means to energize talk on information literacy at an European level, with a specific end goal to advance the foundation of a Culture of information in Europe. They have likewise made the European Observatory on IL Approaches and Exploration. http://www.informationliteracy.org.uk/il-organisations-uk/il-organisations-international/).

IFLA: The International Federation of Library Associations and Institutions (IFLA) have built up a Information Literacy Area. The basic role of the information literacy Segment is to cultivate global collaboration in the advancement of information abilities training in a wide range of libraries and information institutions. They have likewise made InfoLit Worldwide, a database to record data proficiency materials from various parts of the world, in the interest of UNESCO. (http://www.ifla.org/information-literacy).

UNESCO: UNESCO has delivered a simple to-peruse distribution on what information literacy implies. It is intended for occupied open approach creators, business officials, common society executives and honing experts and could along these lines be utilized as a part of backing work. It is called "Understanding Information Literacy: A Primer" and is accessible for downloading in English or French from their site. (http://www.informationliteracy.org.uk/il-organisations-uk/il-organisations-international/).

HEAICS: The Higher Education Academy Information and Computing Sciences (HEAICS), UK subject focus is quick to help the two scholastics and experts in creating understudies IT and data proficiency abilities. The HEAICS runs a few workshops every year on information literacy.

The High-level Colloquium on Information Literacy and Lifelong Learning held at Bibliotheca Alexandrina on November 6-9, 2005 developed the Alexandria Proclamation on Information Literacy and Lifelong Learning. It declares that "Information Literacy and Lifelong Learning are the beacons of the information society, illuminating the courses to development, prosperity and freedom" (http://www.informationliteracy).

SCONUL: The Society of College, National and University Libraries (SCONUL) has a Working Group on Information Literacy, who play a lead part in the advancement of hypothesis and practice in connection to Information Literacy (IL) and its part during the time spent learning in further and advanced education inside the UK (Mishra and Mishra, 2010).

1.9 INFORMATION LITERACY: INDIAN SCENARIO

Information literacy is a key component of, and supporter of deep rooted learning. Since instruction organizations differ generally in mission and understudy body, Data Education Projects are to be outlined and custom-made to address particular issues of the clients as opposed to an endorsed set of criteria.

Powerful usage of Information Literacy is conceivable with effective ILP. Different projects are being utilized as a part of the US, UK and other European nations. Data proficiency programs are as of now in presence in smaller structures in different libraries and data focuses in India, in the types of client training, bibliographic guideline, library research, et cetera.

1.10 INFORMATION LITERACY IN HIGHER LEARNING INSTITUTIONS

In India, information literacy is conferred for the most part at organizations of higher learning. This incorporates user training, library orientation and bibliographic instruction programs which are not sufficiently satisfactory to meet the present information requirement of the students. In universities for research degree programmes, a course on research methodology is included where library research techniques are also included.

Training frameworks and establishments must consider important the difficulties of the information age. The focal subject of higher education institutions (HEIs) in many parts of the world is to create deep rooted students with the scholarly capacities of thinking and basic considering. Any preparation in abilities gave towards this heading not just prompts the utilization of the library frameworks successfully yet in addition increases the value of them.

Based on the literature reviewed and keeping in view the present scenario of higher learning institutions and financial crisis in higher education institutions in India, it is felt that importance should be given to information literacy in higher education institutions. Introducing the electronic information literacy programme in the academic setting is an institutional issue for the university, as well as the library. The University Grants Commission (UGC) has made genuine efforts to improve the higher education system by introducing e-Shodh Sindhu Consortium. INFLIBNET which is the co-coordinating agency for e-Shodh Sindhu Consortium is conducting various training programmes, user awareness programmes, workshops and seminars for research scholars, faculty members and library staff from many universities across the country, on how to access these abundant resources offered by the UGC.

Academic Libraries in India are likewise offering a few information literacy programs.

Sayaji Rao Gaekwad Central Library of Banaras Hindu University has started the information literacy programme, as scheduled every year on the occasion of new sessions, to make students, research scholars and teachers aware of the e-resources available through the Central Library since September 9, 2014. In the first phase of this programme, more than 500 students and research scholars of the Institute of Agricultural Sciences have been trained with the help of computer and multimedia instructions. The Central Library provides more than 1 lakh e-books, approximately 13 thousand e-journals and about 10 databases on various subjects by notable publishers like Sage, Springer, Nature, Web of Knowledge etc for advocacy and research. The Information Literacy Programme is scheduled every year by the Central Library in different subjects to enhance the usefulness of available knowledge.

The Delhi University Library System (DULS) has huge print collections. DULS also subscribes to a valuable number of databases. Besides, DULS researches regularly on open access initiatives to reap the full benefit of Public Domain Electronic Resources. In, addition with a view to educate users and enhance their electronic abilities and make them competent for retrieving precise and relevant through Internet, DULS has offered a regular Information Literacy Programme since 2006. In continuation, DULS has recently organized a two-day training, the Trainers: Workshop on Information Literacy and Competency for University and College Library Professionals

The point is to prepare library and information experts for forward transmission of the aptitudes to end clients.

Jawaharlal Nehru University, Central Library, is an information center for the JNU look into group. The library gives far reaching access to books, journals, thesis, research papers, reports and newspaper sections to the clients. As a piece of Information Literacy Program, the Central Library has sorted out various addresses for staff, scientists and students as a team with different scholastic foundations, distributers and database makers in JNU.

Jamia Milia Islamia University Library has been arranging a information literacy program for freshers and prepared them for computerized assets, i.e. e-journals and other in-house digitized e-resources. The library likewise offers help to visually impaired students through assistive technology.

Jamia Hamdard University Library offers library orientation programs for students and researchers and acquaints them with online journals and databases subscribed by the library through the UGC Infonet Digital Library Consortia.

The Guru Govind Singh Indraprastha University Library has a separate University Information Resource Centre (UIRC). The centre has a number of e-journals, e-books and databases for users for their teaching, study and research activities. UIRC also organizes orientation programmes for the new users in the library.

The Indian Institute of Technology, Delhi Central Library every year organizes orientation and information literacy programmes for undergraduate, postgraduate students and research scholars to access the library e-resources and services.

Delhi Technological University Library has a rich collections of more than 123000 books and several foreign and Indian journals to facilitate the ongoing research activities and to expand the areas of future research activities. The library has prepared a manual to expose new users to the library activities. This manual is provided during the enrolment for members of the library. The manual is also available in the digital library for reference. The library organizes information literacy programmes under the title "explore the library" for the users. (Mishra and Upadhayay, 2015).

1.11 IL PROGRAMMES FOR LIS PROFESSIONALS

The academic staff colleges established in the universities organize regular orientation/refresher courses for teachers and librarians to imbibe the skills for locating and accessing information in the changing environment.

A large number of the Government Division' Library and Information Centres organize orientation programmes for their staff to acquire information access skills.

The national documentation focuses like the National Institute of Science Communication and Information Resources (NISCAIR) and National Social Science Documentation Center (NASSDOC) assume a huge part in orientating library and information science experts of the nation to aquire the abilities of access to information.

At the school level associations like The National Council of Education Research and Training (NCERT) and State Council of Education Research and Training (SCERT) conduct regular orientation programs/refresher courses for school librarians.

1.12 ROLE OF LIBRARY ASSOCIATIONS IN INDIA

Library Associations exist in most of the states and union territories of India apart from those at the national level. State level library associations are very active in the development of public libraries in their respective states.

Some library associations at national level are now proactive in spreading the information literacy competency for librarians and library users. In December 2005, the Indian

Library Association (ILA) organized the 51st All India Conference which was held at Kurukshetra University, Kurukshetra, with the focus on libraries, information literacy and lifelong learning, where many libraries felt the importance of information literacy in lifelong learning and optimizing the usage of information in libraries. At this conference ILA also recommended formation of a National Information Literacy Mission and the National Information Literacy Task Force to implement information literacy competency development programmes throughout the country without further delay.

In October 2005, an International Information Literacy workshop was held at the Punjabi University, Patiala, to promote information literacy in South and South East Asia, with the support of UNESCO and other partners. In September 2003 at Prague, the International Alliance for Information Literacy was formed where India's Networking Alliance for Voluntary Actions (www.navaindia.org), a network of NGOs, became a member. (Ghosh and Das, 2006, p.10)

Objectives of the Study

The main aim of the study is to estimate the level of information literacy in research scholar as well as postgraduate students using libraries in IIT and IIM. The objectives for this research are:

1. To examine the purpose of visits to the library by users.
2. To identify the competency level of information literacy among the users.
3. To identify areas of strengths and weaknesses in information literacy skills among the users.
4. To find out the status of information literacy programmes offered by the libraries.
5. To assess the ability and effectiveness of the users in acquiring the information.

6. To determine the use of various search techniques and strategies.
7. To examine the level of satisfaction among users with the information literacy programmes offered by the libraries.

Hypotheses of the Study

The following hypotheses have been formulated to study and verify the data and facts that will be collected during the survey:

1. The users have considerable awareness about different sources of information.
2. The users have considerable awareness about search strategies and techniques for accessing the required information.
3. Researchers and postgraduate students are able to use appropriate methods as evaluation criteria while selecting the required information for their study purposes.
4. Most of the users have the ability to retrieve the required information from the sources.
5. Research scholars and postgraduate students need more training assistance and guidance on how to use and access electronic and print information resources.
6. The users are reasonably satisfied with the information literacy programmes offered by the libraries.

Scope of the Study

The aim of this study is to understand and test the information literacy skills of graduates as well as research scholars of most sought after institutes namely IITs and IIM's libraries. The study will take into account data from four institutions mentioned below.

1. Indian Institute of Technology, Delhi

2. Indian Institute of Technology, Roorkee
3. Indian Institute of Management, Lucknow
4. Indian Institute of Management, Indore

References

1. Bavakutty, M. and Nasiruddin, T.P.O (2008). "Assessing Information Literacy Competency of Research Students in India: A Case Study," *ICOLIS*, Kaula Lumpur: LISU, FCSIT, pp. 109-121.
2. Bhatt, R.K. (2011). Information Literacy Models and Competencies Development Initiatives in India. *International Conference of Asian Special Libraries Tokyo, Japan*. Vol.11, p. 2013.
3. Biradar, B. S. and Swapna, G. (2011). Information Literacy Competency: A Study of Bioscience Students of Kuvempu University, *8th International CALIBER*, 2011, Goa University, pp. 445-455.
4. Brown, Cecelia M. (1999). Information Literacy of Physical Science Graduate Students in the Information Age. *College and Research Libraries*, pp. 426-438.
5. Crawford, John (2006). Use of Electronic Information Services and Information Literacy: A Glasgow Caledonian University Study, *Journal of Librarianship and Information Science,* Vol. 38 (1), pp. 33-44.
6. Eisenberg, Michael B. (2004). *Information Literacy: Essential Skill for the Information Age*. London: Libraries Unlimited.
7. Ferguson, Jessame E., Teresa Y. Neely and Sullivan, Kathryn (2006). A Basement of Information Literacy of Biology Students. *Reference and User Services Quarterly*. Vol. 46 (2), pp. 67-71.
8. Garner, S. (2003, September). *Information Literacy and Consumer Health: White Paper for Use at the Information Literacy Meeting of Experts*.
9. Ghosh, S. B. and Das, Anup Kumar (2006). Information Literacy Initiative in India with Special Reference to Emerging Knowledge Economy. *International Conference on Information Literacy (ICIL)*, Kula Lumpur, Malaysia, pp. 1-11.

10. Godwin, Peter and Parker, Jo, eds. (2012). *Information Literacy Beyond Library 2.0.* London: Facet Publishing. pp. 23-29.
11. Jamal Uddin,Md and Hasan, Nazrul (2012). Use of Information Technology in Library Service: A Study on Some Selected Libraries in the Northern Part of Bangladesh, *International Journal of Library and Information Science*, Vol. 4 (3), pp. 34-44.
12. Joshi, Manoj Kumar and Sharma, Sanjeev (2009). Students Use of Various Information Sources and Need for Information Literacy in Kurukshetra University, *Library Herald*, Vol. 47 (1), pp. 46-59.
13. Karisiddappa, C. R. and Kavita, H. C. (2004). Information Literacy as a Means of Information Empowerment, *University News*, Vol. 42 (49), pp. 11-15.
14. Khairah, Namarta. *Information Literacy and Continuing Education: A Teacher's Views. Libraries, Information Literacy and Lifelong Learning.* 51st All India Library Conference Papers Kurukshetra, December16-18, 2005, New Delhi: Indian Library Association, 2005, pp. 259-264.
15. Koneru, Indira (2010). ADDIE: Designing Web-Enabled Information Literacy Instructional Modules, *DESIDOC Journal of Library & Information Technology*, Vol. 30 (3), pp. 23-34.
16. Konnur, P.V. (2011). Information literacy in Higher Education: A revolution in learning. (http://hdl.handle.net/123456789/2749)
17. Kutner, Laurie and Armstrong, Alison (2012). Rethinking Information Literacy in a Globalized World. *Communications in Information Literacy*, Vol. 6, (1), 2012 pp. 24-31.
18. Mishra, R. N. and Mishra, C. (2010). Relevance of Information Literacy in a Digital Environment. *Journal of Emerging Trends in Computing and Information Sciences*, Vol. 1(1), pp. 48-54.
19. Mishra, Rajeev and Upadhyay, Ashok Kumar (2015). Information Literacy in India: Enhancing Services to the Research Community in the Digital Environment. *National Conference on Library Information Science and Information Technology for Education*. Modern Rohini Education Society.
20. Mutch, Alistair (2008). *Managing Information and Knowledge in Organizations: A Literacy Approach*, New York: Routledge.

21. Singh, R.K. (2012). Information Seeking Behaviour of Medical Practitioners: A Case Study. *International Journal of Information Research*, Vol. 2 (1), pp. 28-44.
22. Singh,Jnanendra Narayan and Joshi, Taruna (2006). Information Literacy Skills of Undergraduates Students: A Case Study of Sri Venkateswara College, University of Delhi. *NACLIN*, pp. 331-336.
23. Torras, Maria-Carme and Setre, Tove Pemmer (2009). *Information Literacy Education: A Process Approach*, Oxford: Chandos Publishing.
24. Vijayakumar, A. and Vijayan, Sudhi S. (2011). Application of Information Technology in Libraries: A Overview. *International Journal of Digital Library Services*, Vol. 1 (2), pp. 144-149.

2

Research Methodology

2.1. INTRODUCTION

Research is characterized as the discovery of new learning and the utilization of existing information in another, also innovative path in order to create new ideas, techniques and understandings. This could incorporate synthesis and examination of past research to the degree that it prompts new and innovative results.

Research has a significant role to play in this era as it helps in the generation of knowledge. Research is "the more formal, systematic, intensive process of carrying on the scientific method of analysis. It involves a more systematic structure of investigation, usually resulting in a formal record of procedures and a report of results or conclusions" (Best, 1959).

This chapter focuses on the conceptual research design and methodology used in the present study. The methodology used in the present study has been discussed in detail under the following headings:

1. Hypothesis
2. Research Design
3. Research Methodology
4. Research Sample
5. Pilot Survey

6. Data Collection Procedure
7. Data Analysis Method

2.2 HYPOTHESIS

A hypothesis is a clarification for a condition which can be tested somehow which preferably either demonstrates or refutes the speculation. For the span of testing, the hypothesis is taken to be valid, and the objective of the researcher is to thoroughly test the terms of the speculation. The idea of hypothesis is a vital piece of the scientific technique, and it remains constant in different disciplines too.

When somebody details a hypothesis, he or she does as such with the aim of testing it, and the result of potential tests ought to be obscure before the theory is made. While figuring a hypothesis, the beliefs of the scientific method are frequently remembered, in this manner enabling the theory to be testable in a way which could be repeated by other individuals. It is likewise kept clear and basic, and the hypothesis depends on known information and thinking. A speculation does not need to be correct or wrong, but rather the individual figuring the hypothesis has to be set up to test the hypothesis as far as possible. At the point when researchers publish reports which bolster a hypothesis, they frequently detail the means taken to invalidate the theory and additionally the means which affirmed it, to put forth the defense significantly more grounded.

The following hypotheses have been formulated in this study for the verification of data and facts that will be collected during the survey:

1. The users have considerable awareness about different sources of information.
2. The users have considerable awareness about search strategies and techniques for accessing the required information.

3. Researchers and postgraduate students are able to use appropriate methods as evaluation criteria while selecting the required information for their study purposes.
4. Most of the users are capable of retrieving the required information from the sources.
5. Research scholars and postgraduate students need more training assistance and guidance on how to use and access electronic and print information resources.
6. The users are satisfied with the information literacy programmes offered by the libraries.

2.3 RESEARCH DESIGN

A research design is a logical and systematic plan prepared for directing a research study, the methodology and techniques to be adopted for achieving the objectives. It constitutes the framework for the accumulation, estimation and investigation of information. A research design is the program that aides the investigator during the process of gathering, dissecting and translating perceptions. It ""provides a systematic plan of procedure for the researcher to follow."

Application of research methodology is very essential to study and investigate any problem to the point with accuracy based on facts, figures and the state-of-the-art. Methodology has its own implications and significance in scientific investigation, because objectively any research investigation cannot be obtained unless it is carried out in an orderly and planned manner. Scientific investigation involves careful and suitable design, use of standardized tools and tests identifying a sufficient sample by using the sampling technique. There are several methods of collection of data for measuring the performance and quality of libraries. These methods can broadly be grouped into two, namely quantitative and qualitative methods. The qualitative method comprises focus groups, observation, and case study methods. But the latest trend is using both the methods for qualitative study of libraries and information centres. There are many tools available for collecting data such as (i) Observation method (ii) Interview method (iii) Questionnaire method (iv) Schedules (v) Interview by telephone. Each and every tool has its own importance. In the present study, the investigator adopted the questionnaire, observation and interview methods for the collection of data.

2.3.1 Questionnaire Method

The questionnaire is a tool to collect a data from the diverse and widely scattered group. It is called the heart of the survey operation. The most important part in a questionnaire is designing the questionnaire. It is very important to design a questionnaire appropriately to get the desired results. There are two types of questionnaires:

1. Open questionnaire: In this type of questionnaire no answer is given against the question. The respondent provides the answer in his/her own words.
2. Closed questionnaire: In this type of questionnaire, the answer is given against the question. The respondent has to select one of the options written against the question. The questionnaire is given to the respondent concerned and asks for the opinion or factual information. The questions are designed in such a way that the relation of one question to another can be readily apparent to the respondent. The question sequence must be clear and the users have to answer the question at their own level.

In the present investigation, the questionnaire was received for the gathering of information. Two questionnaires were designed, one for the librarian to gather information about the services, resources and information literacy programmes and another for the users of four libraries, i.e. IIT, Delhi, IIT, Roorkee, IIM, Lucknow and IIM, Indore. The users' questionnaires were personally dispersed and gathered from them. The data identified with the library was acclimatized from the librarian through questionnaires. The website and annual reports were likewise counseled.

2.3.2 Interview Method

The interview method is a direct tool of collecting data and has greater flexibility. This method is unique because the collection of data is through direct verbal interaction with the individuals and through telephonic interviews.

The interview method was also used in the present study. Personal conversations with the librarian and the library staff were made at the time of visiting the library. Sometimes, personal talks with the users were also initiated. After collecting the filled-up questionnaires, some telephonic conversations were also made to clarify some of the doubts and questions.

2.3.3 Observation Method

The observation technique involves human or mechanical observation of what people actually do or what events take place during a buying or consumption situation.

The investigator visited the libraries at different working hours spread over a number of days to observe the functioning of the library; resources and services provided in the library, library orientation or information literacy programmes provided by the IIT and IIM libraries and instructions or training provided by the library professionals to the users to access the library resources and services.

2.4. TOOLS USED FOR THE STUDY

In order to undertake this study and conduct a qualitative and quantitative analysis, a combination of the questionnaire technique along with the interview and observation methods were adopted for data collection.

2.5 STRUCTURE OF THE QUESTIONNAIRES

The questionnaire is the most popular method of collecting data for an evolution and assessment. The most important part in a questionnaire is its designing and formulation. It is very important to design a questionnaire appropriately to get the desired results. While designing a questionnaire, it is good to use standardized methodologies, as it allows us to benefit from the experience of others and to compare the results of similar libraries.

Two sets of questionnaire were designed for the use of data collection. One for the librarian to collect data about the library collection, library staff, working hours, category of users, budget, information resources, services, and frequency of ILP, areas of ILP, method and techniques used in the information literacy programme of four respective libraries. It includes about 32 multiple choice, open ended and closed ended questions referring to different aspects of libraries and information literacy. Another questionnaire was designed for the users (research scholars and postgraduate students) dealing with users perception towards the information literacy aspects, information literacy programmes, search techniques and strategies, assessment tools for information literacy competency and users' satisfaction level. It includes about 33 multiple choice, open-ended and close-ended questions referring to various aspects of libraries and information literacy.

2.6. RESEARCH SAMPLE AND POPULATION DESIGN

It is not possible to collect large quantities of data of each and every library users in four libraries under study. Therefore, within each institute the proportionate stratified random sampling method was used for selecting samples. The population was divided into two groups/strata, i.e. postgraduate students and research scholars. The sample size of library users has been limited to approximately 10% of the total populations.

Table 2.1.1:
Institute wise distribution of questionnaires

Categories	Number of Respondents							
	IITD		IITR		IIML		IIMI	
	RS N=200	PGS N=200	RS N=200	PGS N=200	RS N=70	PGS N=200	RS N=70	PGS N=200
Total strength	1597	2985	1352	3168	80	920	106	1117
Questionnaires distributed	300	300	300	300	80	300	106	300
Responses received	224	251	263	276	76	244	94	265
Total response rate	(74.66%)	(83.66%)	(87.66%)	(92%)	(95%)	(81.33%)	(88.67%)	(88.33%)
Questionnaires analysed (selected)	200 (89.28%)	200 (79.68%)	200 (76.04%)	200 (72.46%)	70 (92.10%)	200 (81.96%)	70 (74.46%)	200 (75.47%)

Table 2.1.1 depicts the number of respondents according to institutes. The total strength of research scholars, i.e. 1597 and postgraduate students 2985 in IITD followed by 1352 research scholars and 3168 postgraduate students in IITR, 80 research scholars and 920 postgraduate students in IIML whereas, IIMI has a total strength of research scholars, i.e. 106 and 1117 postgraduate students. A sample of 300 questionnaires distributed among the research scholars and 300 questionnaires were distributed among the postgraduate students of IITD. This followed 300 questionnaires distributed among research scholars and postgraduate students of IITR, 80 questionnaires distributed among research scholars and 300 questionnaires provided to postgraduate students of IIML. Another 106 questionnaires were distributed among research scholars and 300 questionnaires were distributed among postgraduate students of IIMI. Responses received from research scholars, i.e. 224 (74.66%) and from postgraduate students 251 (83.66%) of IITD followed by IITR were received responses from research scholars, i.e. 263 (87.66%) and 276 (92%) from postgraduate students, 76 (95%) received from research scholars and 244 (81.33%) received from postgraduate

students of IIML, 94 (88.67%) received from research scholars and 265 (88.33%) from postgraduate students of IIMI. Finally, on investigation 200 (89.28%) questionnaires were found valid from research scholars and 200 (79.68%) questionnaires from postgraduate students of IITD followed by 200 (76.04%) questionnaires from research scholars and 200 (72.46%) from postgraduate students of IITR, 70 (92.10%) research scholars and 200 (81.96%) postgraduate students of IIML and 70 (74.46%) questionnaires from research scholars and 200 (75.4%) questionnaires from postgraduate students of IIMI were found valid for final analysis of data.

2.6.1 Total No. of Sample Size and Distributions

In all, 1986 questionnaires were administered to the users of selected libraries, of which 1693, i.e. (85.24%) responses were received back from the users. The investigator selected 1340, i.e. (79.14%) responses from the users. Likewise 4 questionnaires were distributed to the librarians/ in-charge Librarians of four libraries, i.e. 100% and all four questionnaires were received back and selected for the analysis of data.

2.7. PILOT SURVEY

A pilot study is a small-scale rehearsal for a larger main study. Pilot surveys fulfil a range of important functions and can provide important insights for researchers. A pilot study was conducted to verify the reliability of the method chosen. The results from the pilot study was integrated into the current section.

A pilot survey was carried out among 100 respondents of the four libraries under study before going into the actual data collection. On the basis of the response of these questionnaires, personal observation and discussions with respondents, some minor corrections were made in the questionnaire for main study.

2.8. DATA COLLECTION

Data serves as the basis or the raw material for analysis. Without the analysis of factual data, no specific inferences can be drawn. The relevance, adequacy, reliability of data determines the quality of findings of the study. Hence, the data is very important for any study.

For collection of data, the investigator personally visited four libraries and approached the librarian, seeking permission to distribute the questionnaire to the users. Questionnaires were personally provided to the users of four respective libraries. Duly filled questionnaires were collected back on the same day or later and were checked for completeness and accorded unique identification numbers and filed for data entry and processing.

The researcher personally consulted the library staff and users, followed by an informal talk regarding information literacy and different aspects of their libraries. Whenever necessary the investigator also conducted an informal interview with the librarians and other library staff to clarify some doubts; in addition, the observation method was also adopted to observe the overall system related to information literacy and different aspects of libraries.

2.9. DATA ANALYSIS AND INTERPRETATION

After processing the data, the investigator needs to analyse it to draw inferences or conclusions. Analysis plan provides insights into the most optimal manner in which the voluminous data collected could be summarized and analysed, to arrive at the answers to the research questions and to address the research objectives (Ramachandran, 1993).

The quantitative and qualitative data collected through the questionnaire, observation method and informal interviews was keyed in excel file and organized and tabulated by using statistical methods, tables and percentage. Statistical analysis of the data was made with the help of the Statistical Package for Social Science (SPSS).

References

1. Best, John W. and James V. Kahn (2005). *Research in Education*, 2nd ed, New Delhi: Pearson.
2. Majhi, Priti Ranajan and Khatua, Prafull Kumar (2013). *Research Methodology: Concepts, Methods, Techniques and SPSS*, Mumbai: Himalaya Publishing House.
3. Ramachandran, P. (1993). *Survey Research for Social Work: A Primer*, Bombay: Institute for Community Organization Research.
4. Ramamurthy, G. C. (2015). *Research Methodology*. New Delhi: Dreamtech.

3

Data Analysis and Interpretation

The problem for the present study is "**Information Literacy Among Users of Select IIT and IIM Libraries: A Comparative Study.**" This chapter deals with analysis and interpretation of data, which have been collected through questionnaires. The researcher visited all the selected IIT and IIM libraries for the study personally and circulated the designed questionnaires to the librarians and the users. The researcher interacted with almost all the librarians and users of the libraries and assisted them in filling the questionnaires. A personal visit to the libraries helped the researcher to gather more information and see the actual services provided by them.

The collected data has been organized and tabulated by simple statistical methods. The purpose of analysis is to shape data to intelligible forms, that the relation of research problems can be studied and tested.

The two questionnaires were designed (details of the questionnaires are given in the appendices I and II) to collect the necessary data regarding the present study. One questionnaire was designed for librarians, which consist of two parts, i.e. Part A and Part B. Part A consists of a brief profile of libraries, i.e. library collections, library staff, library services, software used, library budget, electronic journals, etc. Part B deals with Information Literacy, i.e. library provided IL, ILP for whom, areas of ILP, IL instruction, IL barriers, Information

Literacy Standard, IL assessment tools, etc. It includes 32 open ended and closed ended questions referring to different aspects of libraries and information literacy.

Second, a set of questionnaires was designed for the users (research scholars and postgraduate students) to assess their information literacy skills. The questionnaires included different types of questions such as multiple choices, open ended and closed ended questions referring to different aspects of information literacy.

PART-A

In all, 1986 questionnaires were administered to the users of selected libraries, of which 1693, i.e. (85.24%) responses were received back from the users. The investigator selected 1340, i.e. (79.14%) responses from the users. Likewise 4 questionnaires were distributed to the librarians/In-charge Librarians of four libraries, i.e. 100% and all the four questionnaires were received back and selected for the analysis of data.

The analyzed data is presented in tabular form along with graphs wherever required.

Table 3.1.1: Working Hours of Libraries

Description	IITD	IITR	IIML	IIMI
Number of working days (approximately/ year)	360 days (excluding five national holidays)	353 days	All days (except gazetted holidays)	362 days
Opening hours (working days)	9 am to 9 pm	8:30 am to 10 pm	9 am to 9:30 pm	9 am to 10 pm
Opening hours (Saturdays, Sundays and holidays)	10 am to 6:30 pm	9:45 am to 6:30 pm	12 am to 8:30 pm	2 pm to 10 pm

(IITD= IIT Delhi, IIT=IIT Roorkee,
IIML= IIM Lucknow, IIMI=IIM Indore)

Table 3.1.1 shows that IITD working days are 360 days, followed by IITR working days are 353, IIML is open all days (except gazetted holidays) and IIMI is open 362 days. It can be found that IIMs open more no of days in compare of IITs. IIMI is one of them to open 362 days out of the selected four libraries.

In order to ascertain the position of human resources in the libraries, details of professional and non-professional staff working in four study libraries are collected.

Table 3.1.2: Staff Profile

Designation	IITD	IITR	IIML	IIMI
Librarian/In-charge Librarian	1 (Prof. In-charge, Library)	1	1 (In-charge Librarian)	1
Deputy Librarian	2	-	2	-
Assistant Librarian	4	3	4	1
Information Scientist/Officers	-	-	-	-
Professional Assistants	3	10	2	5
Semi-Professional Assistants	-	3	-	-
Library Assistants	1	4	1	-
Technical Assistants	-	-	-	-
Library Clerks	-	1	-	-
Curators			-	-
Library Attendants	4	2	1	5
Others	3	-	2	4
Total	**18**	**24**	**13**	**16**

The Table 3.1.2 depicts the staff profile of libraries in tabular form. IITR and IIMI have a full time Librarian, whereas IITD and IIML have an In-charge Librarian. Further categorized the strength of total staff in these four libraries, IITR has maximum no of staff (24), whereas (18) in IITD, (16) in IIMI, and 13 staff in IIML.

Table 3.1.3: Library Collection

Library	IITD	IITR	IIML	IIMI
Total Collection	13.2 lakhs (print form) 1.6 lakhs (electronic form)	4.5 lakhs (print form) 65,000 (electronic form)	45,470 (print form) 166,856 (electronic form)	37,878 (print form 2.7 Lakhs (electronic form)

Table 3.1.3 shows that the total collection IITD has the highest, i.e.13.2 lakhs in print form and 1.6 lakhs in clectronic form, followed by IITR has 4.5 lakhs in print form and 65,000 in electronic form. Similarly, IIMI has 37,878 in print form and 2.7 lakhs in electronic form and IIML has 45,470 in print form and 166,856 in electronic form.

It shows that IITD have more collection in compare to IITR, IIML and IIMI.

Table 3.1.4: Library Users' Profile

Registered Library Users	IITD	IITR	IIML	IIMI
Research Scholar	1597	1352	80	106
Postgraduate students	2985	3168	920	1117
Total	**4582**	**4520**	**1000**	**1223**

Table 3.1.4 depicts the user statistics of selected libraries. IITD has the highest number of registered users that is 4582, in which 1597 users are research scholars and 2985 are postgraduate students. IITR has 4520 registered users in which 1352 research scholars and 3168 postgraduate students similarly, IIMI has 1223 registered users in which 106 research scholars and 1117 postgraduate students and IIML has 1000 registered users in which 80 research scholars and 920 postgraduate students registered.

Its shows that in IITs more users are registered in compare to IIMs.

Table 3.1.5: Library Budget

Name of the Library	IITD	IITR	IIML	IIMI
Annual Budget	14.25 crores	15.4 crores	3.75 crores	3.4 crores

Table 3.1.5 clearly indicates the current annual budget (2015-16) of selected libraries. IITD has the highest annual budget i.e. (15.4 crore), where as IITR, i.e. (14.25 crores), IIML, i.e. (3.75 crores), and IIMI has the lowest budget annual budget, i.e. (3.4 crores).

Its shows that in IITs more budget is sanctioned in compare to IIMs.

Table 3.1.6: Library Housekeeping/Automation Software

Library Automation Software	IITD	IITR	IIML	IIMI
SOUL				
KOHA				
LIBSYS	√	√	√	
E-Granthalaya				
New GENLIB				
VIRTUA				√
Other				

Table 3.1.6 shows the library automation software used by the selected libraries. These three libraries, i.e. IITD, IITR, and IIML use automation software LIBSYS only out different Library Automation Software where IIMI using automation software VIRTUA only.

Table 3.1.7: Digital Library Software

Digital Library Software	IITD	IITR	IIML	IIMI
GSDL				
D-Space	√	√		
E-Print				
None			√	√

Table 3.1.7 presents the Digital library software used by the selected libraries. IITD and IITR use D-Space but IIML and IIMI do not use any digital library software.

Table 3.1.8: Number of PC/Workstations

Name of the Library	No. of PC/Workstations
IITD	45
IITR	25
IIML	13
IIMI	15

Table 3.1.8 shows that the highest no of PC/workstations (45) used by the IITD, followed by IITR, IIMI and IIML 25, 15 and 13 respectively.

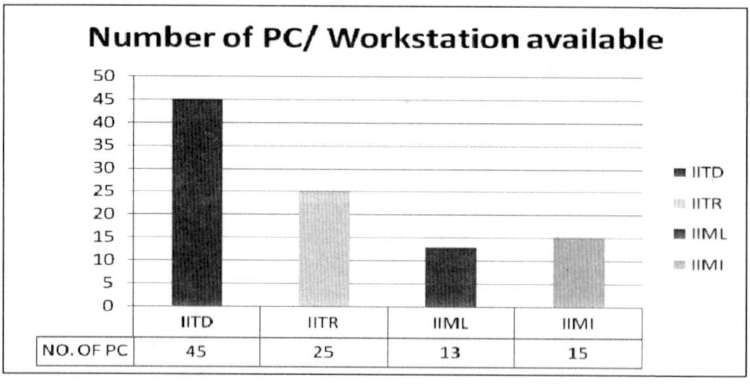

Table 3.1.9: Library Services

Library Services	IITD	IITR	IIML	IIMI
User Education	√	√	√	√
CAS	√	√	√	√
SDI	√	√	√	√
Indexing Services	√	√	√	
Abstracting Services		√	√	
Reprographic Services	√	√	√	√
Translation Services				
Referral Services	√	√	√	√
Literature Search Services	√	√	√	√
Any Other				

Table 3.1.9 depicts the services provided by the selected libraries. Most of the services are provided by these libraries. Translation service is not provided by selected libraries. The IITD and IIMI do not provide abstracting service to their users.

Table 3.1.10: Library Network

Library Network	IITD	IITR	IIML	IIMI
DELNET	√	√	√	√
INFLIBNET	√			√
BONET				
ADINET				
CALIBNET				
SIRNET				

Table 3.1.10 shows these selected libraries associated with Library Networks. These selected libraries are members of DELNET whereas only IITD and IIMI are members of INFLIBNET.

Table 3.1.11: Participating in any Consortia for Electronic Journals

Consortia	IITD	IITR	IIML	IIMI
J-gate/JCCC				
EBSCO	√			
JSTOR				
E-Sodh Sindhu	√	√	√	√
FORSA				
CSIR Library Consortia				

Table 3.1.11 depicts the selected libraries are connected with electronic journals consortia. Indeed, it is encouraging to know that all the libraries are connected with E-Sodh Sindhu consortia, whereas only IITD is also associated with EBSCO e-journals consortia.

PART-B (INFORMATION LITERACY)

Table 3.2.1: Libraries Provide Information Literacy

Information Literacy	IITD	IITR	IIML	IIMI
Yes	√	√	√	√
No				
If yes, since when?	Since establishment of the Library	Since 2007	Since 1984	Since 2001

It is clear from Table 3.2.1 that these four selected libraries provide Information Literacy (IL). It reveals that IITD is the oldest to start IL since 1961, establishment of the library followed by IIML began since 1984, whereas IIMI started since 2001 and IITR started IL since 2007.

Information Literacy Programmes (ILP) are already provided in various libraries and information centres in India, ILP in the form of such as user education, library orientation, bibliographic instruction, and library instruction, etc. All these selected libraries have conducted ILP for their users. Table 3.2.2

Table 3.2.2: Information Literacy Programmes

ILP for Whom	IITD	IITR	IIML	IIMI
Research Scholars	√	√	√	√
Postgraduate Students	√	√	√	√
Undergraduate Students	√	√		
Faculty	√		√	
Administrative Staff	√		√	

reveals that the IITD has offered ILP for research scholars, postgraduate students, faculty, and administrative staff, followed by IIML has offered ILP for research scholars, postgraduate students, faculty and administrative staff, IITR has provided ILP for research scholars, postgraduate students, and undergraduate students, whereas IIMI has offered ILP for research scholars, and postgraduate students only.

Table 3.2.3: How To Conduct Ilp, As Per

ILP As per	IITD	IITR	IIML	IIMI
Department- wise				
Faculty-wise				
Class-wise				
Subject-wise				
Common for all categories of users	√	√	√	√
Other				

Table 3.2.3 depicts that all four libraries, i.e. IITD, IITR, IIML, and IIMI have conducted information literacy programmes as common for all categories of users.

Table 3.2.4 presents the librarian's prior agenda while organizing Information Literacy Programmes (ILP) in these selected libraries. IITD is the prior agenda while organizing ILP to attract students towards the library and optimize the usage of library resources followed by IITR and IIML has prior

Table 3.2.4:
As a Librarian what is the prior agenda while organizing ILP?

Purpose of ILP	IITD	IITR	IIML	IIMI
To attract students towards the library	√	√	√	
To optimize the usage of library resources	√	√	√	
To prepare students for group discussion				
Ability to retrieve data for their assignments, efficiently		√	√	√
Other				

agenda while organizing ILP to attract students towards the library, optimize the usage of library resources, and ability to retrieve data for their assignment efficiently. IIMI has one prior agenda while organizing ILP to develop the ability to retrieve data for their assignments efficiently.

Table 3.2.5: Changed or Modified Courses to Increase Awareness and Knowledge of Information Literacy Standard

ILP Courses	IITD	IITR	IIML	IIMI
Yes	√		√	
No		√		√
If yes…how	Added lecture/discussion Added new assignment		Added lecture/discussion	

For maximum utilization of such vast and huge information resources the information literacy skills is the need of the hour. Table 3.2.5 shows the changed or modified ILP course to increase awareness and knowledge information literacy standards. It was found that IITD and IIML have changed the ILP course and added lecture/discussion and new assignments to increase awareness and knowledge of information literacy standards. Similarly, IITR and IIMR have not changed the ILP course to increase awareness and knowledge of information literacy standards.

Table 3.2.6:
Barriers to Incorporate Information Literacy Standard into Courses

Barriers	IITD	IITR	IIML	IIMI
Not enough time in the course to add extra content	√			
Don't know how these standards relate to the content of my course				
Don't have enough expertise to discussion the information literacy standards				
Lack of student interest	√		√	√
Students vary in technology expertise				
Not part of the curriculum			√	√
None		√		

Table 3.2.6 shows that barriers incorporate information literacy standards into the courses. The table found that IITD has not enough time in the course to add extra content and lack of student interest to incorporate Information Literacy Standards. Similarly, IIML and IIMI libraries found some barriers, i.e. lack of student interest and ILP was not part of the curriculum. IITR has not found any barrier when trying to incorporate information literacy standards into the course.

Table 3.2.7: International Information Literacy Standard use in ILP

International Information Literacy Standards	IITD	IITR	IIML	IIMI
AASL		√		
ACRL				
ISET				
Other (please specify)				
None	√		√	√

Table 3.2.7 reveals that IITR used the American Association of School Libraries (AASL) International Standard in

Information Literacy Programmes (ILP), whereas IITD, IIML, and IIMI libraries were not used any International Standards in ILP.

Table 3.2.8:
Assessment Tools to Determine Information Literacy Competency

Assessment Tools	IITD	IITR	IIML	IIMI
Yes			√	
No	√	√		√
If yes, (please specify) Other			√	

Table 3.2.8 shows that IIML has an assessment tool to determine student information literacy competency. Similarly, IITD, IITR, and IIMI have not any assessment tools to determine student information competency.

Table 3.2.9:
Information Literacy Instructions During the Last One Year

IL Instructions	IITD	IITR	IIML	IIMI
Library orientation	√	√	√	√
Guided library tour	√	√	√	√
Introductory information skills (i.e. catalogue instruction, introduction to the library website)	√	√	√	√
Advanced information skills (i.e. database training, advanced internet searching)	√	√	√	√
Research-level skills (i.e. conducting literature search, reference style, scholarly publishing, etc.)	√	√	√	√

Information Literacy Instruction was provided in selected libraries during the last one year. Table 3.2.9 clearly indicates that IITD, IITR, IIML, and IIMI libraries provided information literacy instruction, i.e. library orientation, guided library tour, introductory information skills (i.e. catalogue instruction, introduction to the library website), advanced information skills (i.e. database training, advanced internet searching), research-level skills (i.e. conducting literature search, reference style, scholarly publishing, etc.) to the users.

Table 3.2.10: Topics Covered in IL Instruction Programmes

Topic of IL Instructions	IITD	IITR	IIML	IIMI
Introduction to library resources, services, and policies	√	√		√
OPAC/Library catalogue instructions	√	√	√	√
Library website introduction	√	√	√	√
Identification of their own information needs	√	√		
Online searching techniques	√	√	√	√
Use of databases	√	√	√	
Use of search engines	√	√		
Evaluation of information	√	√		
Plagiarism awareness/ethical use of information	√	√	√	√
Copyright	√	√	√	
Citation of information (reference style)	√	√	√	√
Use of citation management software (EndNote, RefWorks, etc)	√	√		
Scholarly publishing	√	√	√	
Other topics				

All four selected libraries have covered different topics in information literacy instruction. It is can be seen from Table 3.2.10 that IITD and IITR libraries covered all related topics in information literacy instructions. Similarly, IIML and IIMI libraries covered topics in information literacy instruction slightly less.

Table 3.2.11 shows that IITD, IITR and IIML libraries were provided information literacy instruction whenever asked to do so, new session/first-time users, and at a specific time after the installation or acquisition of a new system or information sources and also required for the students, whereas IIMI

Table 3.2.11: Provide IL Instructions

IL Instruction provide	IITD	IITR	IIML	IIMI
Whenever asked to do so	√	√	√	√
To new session/first-time users	√	√	√	√
IL is a required course for students	√			
At specific time after the installation or acquisition of a new system or information sources	√	√	√	
Other				

provided IL instructions whenever asked and for the first time users only.

Table 3.2.12: IL Instruction Methods

Methods	IITD	IITR	IIML	IIMI
Face-to-face	√	√	√	√
Workshop/seminars	√	√	-	√
Online/web-based tutorials	√	-	-	√
Combination of online and face to face	-	√	-	√
Printed training manuals	-	√	-	√
Individual instruction at the reference desk	√	√	√	√
Other	-	-	-	-

Table 3.2.12 indicates that IL instruction methods were used by the selected libraries. It is clear from Table 3.2.12 that IIMI used all IL instruction methods, i.e. face-to-face, workshop/ seminars, online/web-based tutorials, combination of online and face-to-face, printed training manuals, individual instruction at the reference desk for the users. Similarly, IITD used IL instruction methods, i.e. face-to-face, workshop/ seminars, online/web-based tutorials, individual instruction at the reference desk and IITR provided IL instruction, i.e. face-to-face, workshop/seminars, online/web-based tutorials,

combination of online and face-to-face, printed training manuals, individual instruction at the reference desk, whereas IIML used only two IL instruction methods, i.e. face-to-face and individual instruction at the reference desk for their users. It indicates that the majority of libraries, i.e. IIMI, IITR, and IITD felt that providing better information literacy instruction methods to the users would increase the proper utilization of library resources and services.

Table 3.2.13: Assess Effectiveness of IL Instruction Session

Methods	IITD	IITR	IIML	IIMI
Yes		√	√	
No	√			√
If yes, then which of the methods used for assessing effectiveness of IL instruction session		a. Quizzes b. Multiple choice questions c. Written feedback d. Oral feedback	a. Quizzes b. Written feedback c. Oral feedback	

Table 3.2.13 shows how to assess the effectiveness of IL instruction session in the four selected libraries. It is observed that IITR and IIML libraries have used a number of methods to assess the effectiveness of IL instruction sessions among the users. Similarly, IITD and IIMI have not used any methods to assess the effectiveness of IL instruction session among the users.

Table 3.2.14: ILP Consultation with Teachers

ILP	IITD	IITR	IIML	IIMI
Yes	√			
No		√	√	√

Table 3.2.14 shows the ILP have developed in consultation with teachers in these four selected libraries. It clearly indicates that IITD has developed ILP in consultation with teachers,

whereas IITR, IIML, and IIMI have not developed ILP in consultation with the teachers.

Table 3.2.15: Responsible for Conducting ILP

Responsible for conducting ILP	IITD	IITR	IIML	IIMI
Librarian	√	√	√	√
Faculty				
Both librarian and faculty in collaboration				
Other				

Table 3.2.15 depicts that, who responsible for conducting information literacy programmes in the selected libraries. It is clearly indicates from Table 3.2.15 that the librarian is mainly responsible for conducting information literacy programmes in all four selected libraries.

PART-C

In all, 1986 questionnaires sheets were administered to the users of selected libraries, of which 1693, i.e. (85.24%) responses were received back from the users. The investigator randomly selected 1340, i.e. (79.14%) responses from the users for analysis of data.

Table 3.3.1 depicts the number of respondents according to institutes. Total strength of research scholars, i.e. 1597 and postgraduate students 2985 in IITD followed by 1352 research scholars and 3168 postgraduate students in IITR, 80 research scholars and 920 postgraduate students in IIML whereas, IIMI has total strength of research , i.e. 106 and 1117 postgraduate students. A sample of 300 questionnaires were distributed among the research scholars and 300 questionnaires were distributed among the postgraduate students of IITD, followed by 300 questionnaires were distributed among research scholars and postgraduate students of IITR, 80 questionnaires were distributed among research scholars and 300 questionnaires

Table 3.3.1: Institute-wise Distribution of Questionnaires

Categories	Number of Respondents							
	IITD		IITR		IIML		IIMI	
	RS N=200	PGS N=200	RS N=200	PGS N=200	RS N=70	PGS N=200	RS N=70	PGS N=200
Total strength	1597	2985	1352	3168	80	920	106	1117
Questionnaires distributed	300	300	300	300	80	300	106	300
Response received	224	251	263	276	76	244	94	265
Total response rate	(74.66%)	(83.66%)	(87.66%)	(92%)	(95%)	(81.33%)	(88.67%)	(88.33%)
Questionnaires analyzed (selected)	200 (89.28%)	200 (79.68%)	200 (76.04%)	200 (72.46%)	70 (92.10%)	200 (81.96%)	70 (74.46%)	200 (75.47%)

were distributed among postgraduate students of IIML and 106 questionnaires were distributed among research scholars and 300 questionnaires were distributed among postgraduate students of IIMI. Responses received from research scholars i.e. 224 (74.66%) and from postgraduate students 251 (83.66%) of IITD followed by IITR received responses from research scholars, i.e. 263 (87.66%) and 276 (92%) from postgraduate students, 76 (95%) received from research scholars and 244 (81.33%) received from postgraduate students of IIML, 94 (88.67%) received from research scholars and 265 (88.33%) from postgraduate students of IIMI. Finally, the investigator 200 (89.28%) questionnaires were found valid from research scholars and 200 (79.68%) questionnaires from postgraduate students of IITD followed by 200 (76.04%) questionnaires from research scholars and 200 (72.46%) from postgraduate students of IITR, 70 (92.10%) research scholars and 200 (81.96%) postgraduate students of IIML and 70 (74.46%) questionnaires from research scholars and 200 (75.4%) questionnaires from postgraduate students of IIMI were found valid for final analysis of data.

Table number 3.3.2 reveals the frequency of visits to the library by respondent Research Scholars (RS) and PG students (PGS). It can be seen from the data that majority of researchers in IIMI (55.71%) visit to the Library daily, similarly in IIML (52.85%), IITD (48.5%) and IITR (43.5%). It can also be seen from table that majority of PGS in IITD (26%) visit to the library daily, similarly in IIML (23.5%), IITR (22.7%) and IIMI (22.5%).

Moreover, majority of PGS (56.5%) in IIML visit to the library weekly and PGS (54%) in IITR, (49%) in IIMI, (45.5%) in IITD. Whereas, researcher (27.5%) in IITD, (25%) in IITR, (24.28%) in IIML, (21.4%) in IIMI stated that they made visit weekly to the library.

It is also visible from the table that monthly visit to the library by RS of IITR (21.5%) is more than RS of IITD (16.5%), IIML (12.87%) and IIMI (18.57%).

Table 3.3.2 Frequency of Visits to the Library

Frequency	IITD		IITR		IIML		IIMI	
	RS N=200	PGS N=200	RS N=200	PGS N=200	RS N=70	PGS N=200	RS N=70	PGS N=200
Daily	97 (48.5%)	52 (26%)	87 (43.5%)	45 (22.7%)	37 (52.85%)	47 (23.5%)	39 (55.71%)	45 (22.5%)
Weekly	55 (27.5%)	91 (45.5%)	50 (25%)	108 (54%)	17 (24.28%)	113 (56.5%)	15 (21.44%)	98 (49%)
Monthly	33 (16.5%)	37 (18.5%)	43 (21.5%)	30 (15%)	9 (12.87)	25 (12.5%)	13 (18.57%)	39 (19.5%)
Occasionally	15 (7.5%)	20 (10%)	20 (10%)	17 (8.5%)	7 (10%)	15 (12.5%)	3 (4.28%)	18 (9%)
Mean	50	50	50	50	17.5	50	17.5	50
SD	35.35	30.30	27.80	40.32	13.70	44.08	15.26	34.03

(Figures within parenthesis represent percentage)

From table it is reflected that monthly visit to the library by PGS of IIMI (19.5%) is more in comparison of PGS of IIML (18.57%), PGS of IITD (18.5%) and PGS of IITR (15%).

Whereas, only a very small percentage of researcher (7.5%) in IITD, (10%) in IITR, (10%) in IIML, (4.28%) in IIMI and PGS (10%) in IITD, (8.5%) in IITR, (12.5%) in IIML, (9%) in IIMI stated that they visit to the library occasionally.

Statistical Inference

It is observed from table number 3.3.2 that maximum number of researchers declared, their frequency of visiting the library is daily i.e. 97, 87, 37, 39 from IITD, IITR, IIML and IIMI which was found to be fairly above their corresponding mean value of 50 (SD=35.35), 50 (SD= 27.80), 17.5 (SD= 13.70), 17.5 (SD= 15.26) respectively. And maximum number of PG Students declared, their frequency of visiting the library is weekly i.e. 91, 108, 113, 98 from IITD, IITR, IIML and IIMI which was found

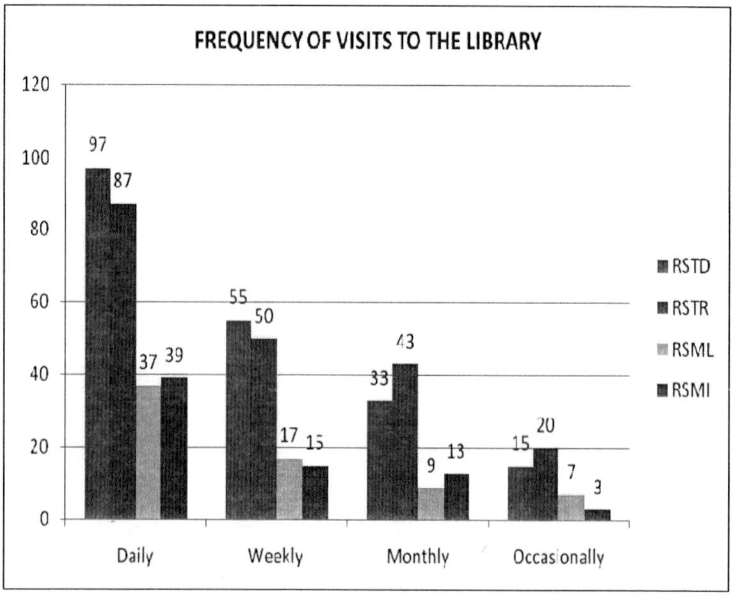

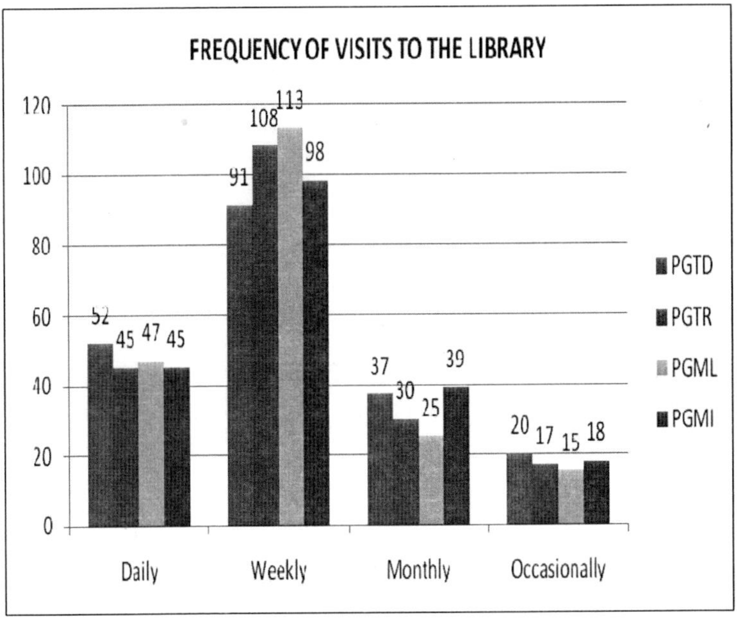

to be fairly above their corresponding mean value of 50(SD= 30.30),50(SD= 40.32), 50(SD= 44.08), 50(SD= 34.03) respectively.

Furthermore, least numbers of respondents visit the library monthly and occasionally which shows lowest point from the mean scores.

Table number 3.3.2 shows that frequency of majority of Research Scholars to visit the library daily, while a contrast was observed in case of PG students that frequency of majority are visiting the library weekly.

Correlation Table also shows that frequency of visits to the library of IITs RS (.987), IITs PGS (.987) is more than frequency of visits to the library IIMs RS (.974), IIMs PGS (.985)

Table number 3.3.3 clearly shows that the major purpose of information needed by the RS in different institutions admitted using information needed for research work, (71.5%), (69%), (70%) and (68.57%) in IITD, IITR,IIML and IIMI

Table 3.3.3: Purpose of Information Needed

Purpose	IITD		IITR		IIML		IIMI	
	RS N=200	PGS N=200	RS N=200	PGS N=200	RS N=70	PGS N=200	RS N=70	PGS N=200
Research work	143 (71.5%)	51 (25.5%)	138 (69%)	54 (27%)	49 (70%)	41 (20.5%)	48 (68.57%)	37 (18.5%)
To publish research papers	88 (44%)	42 (21%)	79 (39.5%)	32 (16%)	24 (34.28%)	26 (13%)	38 (54.28%)	21 (10.5%)
Assignment	53 (26.5%)	98 (49%)	38 (19%)	81 (40.5%)	18 (25.71%)	98 (49%)	14 (20%)	57 (28.5%)
Study purposes	61 (30.5%)	145 (72.5%)	64 (32%)	92 (46%)	21 (30%)	112 (56%)	19 (27.14%)	63 (31.5%)
Attending seminar/workshop	69 (34.5%)	41 (20.5%)	62 (31%)	25 (12.5%)	38 (54.28%)	12 (6%)	25 (35.71 %)	69 (34.5%)
Recreational knowledge	38 (19%)	64 (32%)	21 (10.5%)	33 (16.5%)	26 (37.14%)	39 (19.5%)	11 (15.71%)	28 (14%)
General knowledge	21 (10.5%)	31 (15.5%)	15 (7.5%)	21 (10.5%)	15 (21.42%)	28 (14%)	17 (24.28%)	26 (13%)
Mean	67.57	67.43	59.57	48.29	27.29	50.86	24.57	43.00
SD	39.60	40.63	41.82	28.28	12.08	38.40	13.62	19.60

(Figures within parenthesis represent percentage) (Multiple responses were permitted)

respectively,. Table data also shows low percentage of information needed by PG students, (27%) in IITR, (25.5%) in IITD, (29.5%) in IIML and (18.5%) in IIMI, admitted using information needed for research work.

Furthermore, it founds that a higher percentage of researchers in IIMI (54.28%) accepted that the major purpose of information needed to publish research papers than IITD (44%), IITR (39.4%) and IIML (34.28%) information needed to publish research papers.

Researchers and PG students work always involves keeping abreast of the recent developments in their respective fields and it can be clearly depicted from the table 3.3.3 that, a percentage of the researchers from the select institutes under the study acknowledged using purpose of information needed by the RS to be research work for Assignment i.e. (26.50%) in IITD, (19%) in IITR, (25.71%) in IIML and (20%) in IIMI.

Furthermore, it founds that a higher percentage of PG students of IITD (72.5%) accepted that the major purpose of information needed to study purpose, PGS of IITR (46%), IIML (56%) and IIMI (31.5%).

It can be seen from the data that (54.28%) RS in IIML, accepted that the major purpose of information needed to attend seminar/workshop is higher, (34.5%) in IITD, (31%) in IITR and (35.71%) in IIMI. The data further reveals that the use of the major purpose of information needed to attending seminar/workshop by PG students of IIMI (34.5%) was more on priority as compared to PG students (20.5%) in IITD, (12.5%) in IITR and (6%) in IIML admitted purpose of information needed to attending seminar/workshop.

Whereas, in case of Recreational knowledge (37.14%) RS in IIML was higher than (19%) in IITD, (10.5%) in IITR and 15.71%) in IIMI accepted purpose of information needed for the purpose of Recreational knowledge.

It can be seen from the data that (32%) PG students of IITD use of the major purpose of information needed of Recreational knowledge is higher than PGS, (16.5%) in IITR, (19.5%) in IIML and (14%) in IIMI accepted purpose of information needed for the purpose of Recreational knowledge.

It can be seen from data that (24.28%) RS in IIMI use of the major purpose of information needed of General knowledge is higher in compare to (10.5%) RS in IITD, (7.5%) RS in (IITR), and (21.42) RS in IIML accepted purpose of information needed for the purpose of General Knowledge.

Whereas, only a very small percentage of PG students (15.5%) in IITD, (10.5%) in IITR, (14%) in IIML and (13%) in IIMI stated that purpose of information needed for General Knowledge.

Statistical Inference

The majority of RS purpose of information needed for Research work moreover (71.5%) in IITD, in IITR (69%), IITML (70%) and IIMI (68.57%). Similarly in case of PG students purpose of information needed for Study Purpose moreover (72.5%) in IITD, (46%) in IITR, (56%) in IIML and (31.5%) in IIMI.

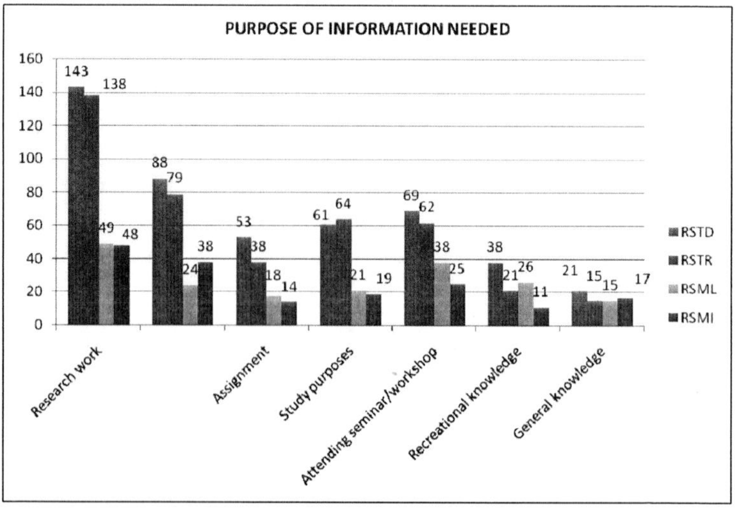

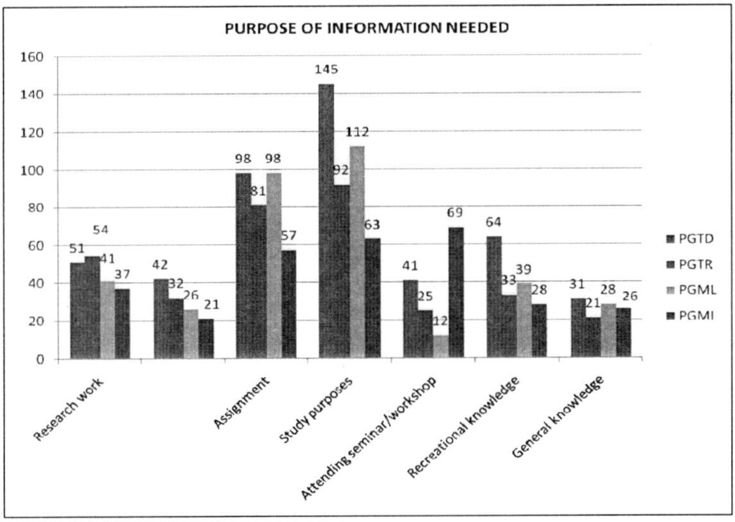

Correlation Table also shows that PURPOSE OF INFORMATION NEEDED of IITs RS (.988), IITs PGS (.924) is more than purpose of information needed IIMs RS (.722), IIMs PGS (.453). IIMs PG correlation is less than 50% which shows PG students are not much interested for information needed.

Table 3.3.4 shows the awareness of research scholars and postgraduate students with different sources of information which were frequently used by them. The data reveals that text books were frequently used by research scholars of IIMI, i.e. 39 (55.71%), 101 (50.5%) of IITR, 31 (44.28%) IIML, and 86 (43%) of IITD while the majority of the postgraduate students of IITD, i.e. 181 (90.5%), 177 (88.5%) of IIMI, 172 (86%) of IIML and 165 (82.5%) of IITR used textbooks for their course work. Research scholars of IITD, i.e. 158 (79%) more than IIMI 51(72.85%), IITR 133 (66.5%), and IIML 41 (58.57%) observed that conference and seminar papers were the best sources to collect the information while the majority of the postgraduate students of IIML, i.e. 91 (45.5%) than IIMI 88 (44%), IITD 87 (43.5%), and IITR 83 (41.5%) used the conference and seminar proceedings. The study indicates that the majority of the research scholars of IITR, i.e. 181 (90.5%) more than IITD 167

Table 3.3.4: Frequently Used Information Sources

Information Sources	IITD		IITR		IIML		IIMI	
	RS N=200	PGS N=200	RS N=200	PGS N=200	RS N=70	PGS N=200	RS N=70	PGS N=200
Textbooks	86 (43%)	181 (90.5%)	101 (50.5%)	165 (82.5%)	31 (44.28%)	172 (86%)	39 (55.71%)	177 (88.5%)
Reference books	114 (57%)	123 (61.5%)	122 (61%)	118 (59%)	35 (50%)	154 (77%)	41 (58.57%)	132 (66%)
Journals	132 (66%)	85 (42.5%)	129 (64.5%)	81 (40.5%)	41 (58.57%)	109 (54.5%)	52 (74.28%)	98 (49%)
Newsletters	98 (49%)	74 (37%)	88 (44%)	56 (28%)	23 (32.85%)	86 (43%)	19 (27.14%)	45 (22.5%)
Theses/ Dissertations	175 (87.5%)	73 (36.5%)	157 (78.5%)	78 (39%)	43 (61.42%)	87 (43.5%)	39 (55.71%)	71 (35.5%)
Conference/ seminar proceedings	158 (79%)	87 (43.5%)	133 (66.5%)	83 (41.5%)	41 (58.57%)	91 (45.5%)	51 (72.85%)	88 (44%)
Wikipedia	88 (44%)	88 (44%)	97 (48.5%)	71 (35.5%)	28 (40%)	52 (26%)	12 (17.14%)	55 (27.5%)
Online Databases/E-journals/ E-books, etc	167 (83.5%)	172 (86%)	181 (90.5%)	157 (78.5%)	45 (64.28%)	162 (81%)	54 (77.14%)	189 (94.5%)
Mean	127.25	110.38	126.00	101.13	35.88	114.13	38.38	106.88
SD	36.06	43.68	31.55	40.88	7.92	43.39	15.44	54.16

(Multiple answers permitted)

(83.5%), IIMI 54 (77.14%) and IIML 45 (64.28%) observed that online databases, e-journals and e-books were the best sources while the majority of the postgraduate students of IIMI, i.e. 189 (94.5%) more than IITD 172 (86%), IIML 162 (81%) and IITR 157 (78.5%) used online databases for their study. Thus, the most used information source was online databases (94.5%), while the least used source was newsletters (17.14%).

Statistical Inference

The majority of RS frequently used information sources for theses/Dissertation moreover (87.5%) in IITD, in IITR (73.5%), IIML (61.42%) and IIMI (55.71%). The majority of PG students frequently used information sources for Textbooks (90.5%) in IITD, (82.5%) in IITR, (86%) in IIML and (88.5%) in IIMI.

Before accessing the information literacy skills of the research scholars and postgraduate students of the selected libraries, it is necessary to know from users whether they are familiar with information literacy. It is clear from Table 3.3.3

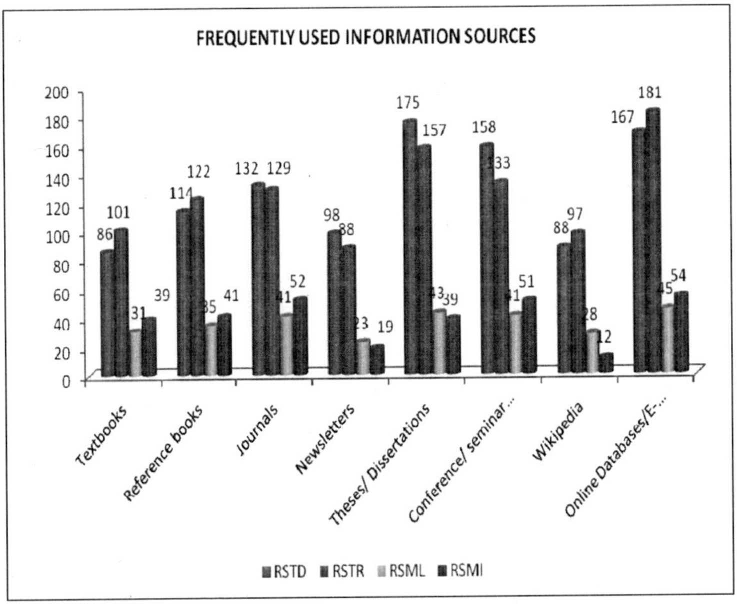

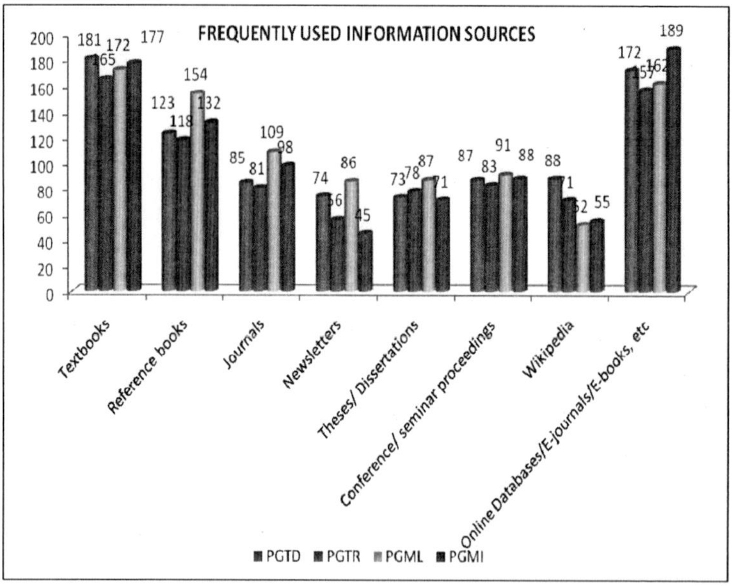

Table 3.3.5: Familiarity with Information Literacy

Response	IITD		IITR		IIML		IIMI	
	RS N=200	PGS N=200	RS N=200	PGS N=200	RS N=70	PGS N=200	RS N=70	PGS N=200
Yes	140 (70%)	154 (77%)	164 (82%)	119 (59.5%)	49 (70%)	137 (68.5%)	41 (58.57%)	129 (64.5%)
No	60 (30%)	46 (23%)	36 (18%)	81 (40.5%)	21 (30%)	63 (31.5%)	29 (41.43%)	71 (35.5%)
Mean	100.00	100.00	100.00	100.00	35.00	100.00	35.00	100.00
SD	56.57	76.37	90.51	26.87	19.80	52.33	8.49	41.01

(If You Take Only Yes, Then SD will not be Calculated)

that research scholars 140 (70%) and postgraduate students 154 (77%) of IITD were familiar with information literacy, while 60 (30%) of the research scholars and 46 (23%) postgraduate students were not familiar with information literacy. In IITR, 164 (82%) research scholars and 119 (59.5%) postgraduate students were familiar with information literacy, while 36 (18%) of the research scholars and 81 (40.5%) postgraduate students were not. 49 (70%) of research scholars and 137 (68.5%) of postgraduate students of IIML were familiar with information literacy, while 21 (30%) of research scholars and 63 (31.5%) postgraduate students were not.

Statistical Inference

Majority of IITR RS respond "familiarity with information literacy" is maximum (82%), IITD RS and IIML RS (69%), IIMI (58.57%). In contrast, IITD PG students familiarity with information literacy moreover (77%), (59.5%) in IITR, (68.5%) in IIML and (64.5%) in IIMI.

Table 3.3.6 depicts that the majority of the research scholars of IITD 61.5%, 60% of IIML, 58.57% of IIMI and 46% of IITR rated their skills highly for accessing information in print format. The majority of the postgraduate students of IITD 61%,

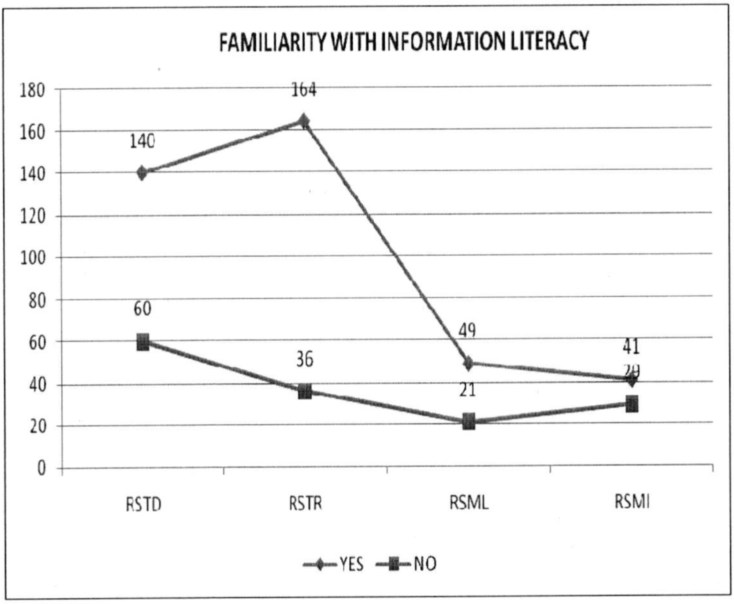

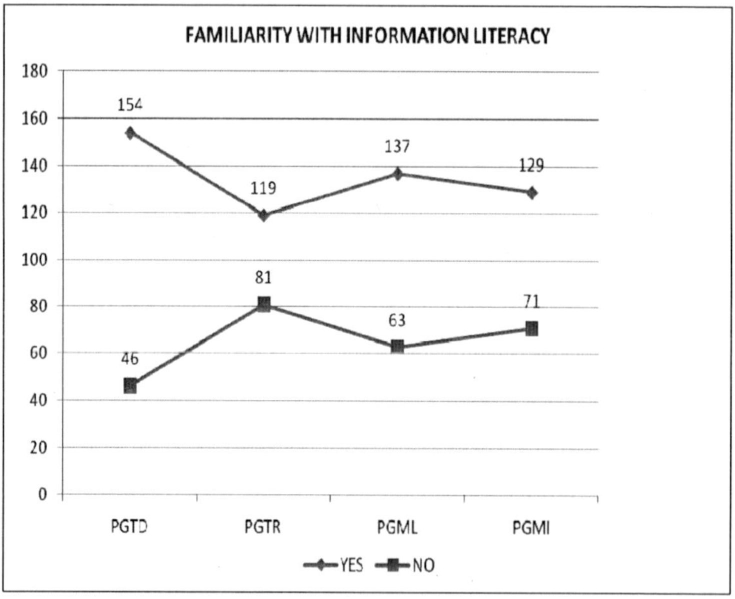

56.5% of IIML, 53.5% of IIMI and 48.5% of IITR rated their skills highly for accessing information in print format.

For accessing information in electronic format, most of the research scholars of IIML and IIMI 57.14%, 45% of IITR and 44.5% of IITD rated their skills highly whereas most of the research scholars of IITR 39.5%, 37% of IITD, 34.28% of IIML and 30% of IIMI rated their skills as average. On the other hand, a high percentage of the postgraduate students of IIMI 57.14%, 51% of IIML 46% of IITR and 42% of IITD rated their skills highly for accessing accurate information in electronic format. It is clear from the table that for accessing information in print format, the majority of the research scholars and postgraduate students rated their skills highly. For accessing information in electronic format, a high percentage of research scholars rated their skills highly, whereas most of the postgraduate students rated their skills as average except for IITR.

Table 3.3.6 Ability to Access Information in Different Formats

Medium	IITD						IITR						IIML						IIMI					
	RS N=200			PGS N=200			RS N=200			PGS N=200			RS N=70			PGS N=200			RS N=70			PGS N=200		
	H	A	L	H	A	L	H	A	L	H	A	L	H	A	L	H	A	L	H	A	L	H	A	L
Print	123 (61.5%)	60 (30%)	17 (8.5%)	122 (61%)	61 (30.5%)	17 (8.5%)	92 (46%)	76 (38%)	32 (16%)	97 (48.5%)	66 (33%)	37 (18.5%)	42 (60%)	21 (30%)	7 (10%)	113 (56.5%)	55 (27.5%)	32 (16%)	41 (58.57%)	23 (32.85%)	6 (8.57%)	107 (53.5%)	69 (34.5%)	24 (12%)
Electronic	89 (44.5%)	74 (37%)	37 (18.5%)	84 (42%)	87 (43.5%)	29 (14.5%)	90 (45%)	79 (39.5%)	31 (15.5%)	92 (46%)	76 (38%)	32 (16%)	40 (57.14%)	24 (34.28%)	6 (8.57%)	102 (51%)	68 (34%)	30 (15%)	40 (57.14%)	21 (30%)	9 (12.85%)	104 (52%)	71 (35.5%)	25 (12.5%)
Mean	106.00	67.00	27.00	103.00	74.00	23.00	91.00	77.50	31.50	94.50	71.00	34.50	41.00	22.50	6.50	107.50	61.50	31.00	40.50	22.00	7.50	105.50	70.00	24.50
SD	24.04	9.90	14.14	26.87	18.38	8.49	1.41	2.12	0.71	3.54	7.07	3.54	1.41	2.12	0.71	7.78	9.19	1.41	0.71	1.41	2.12	2.12	1.41	0.71

H=High, A=Average, L=Low

Statistical Inference

RS and PG students of IITD, IITR, IIML and IIMI prefer Print medium to access information.

Table 3.3.7 shows the level of computer literacy skills of the research scholars and postgraduate students of selected libraries. Most of the research scholars of IIML and IIMI (58.57%), IITD (56%), and IITR (54.5%) rated their skills highly in print document files, while majority of the postgraduate students of IIML (57%), IIMI (54%), IITD (52%) and IITR (51%) rated their skills highly. On the other hand, most of the research scholars of IITR (62.5%), IIML (61.42%), IIMI (58.57%) and IITD (51.5%) rated their skills highly in opening and save files in the computer. For making spreadsheets, the majority of the research scholars of IIMI (61.42%), IIML (58.58%), IITR (54.5%) and IITD (56%) rated their skills highly whereas postgraduate students of IIML (58.58%), IIMI (55%), IITR (49.5%), and IITD (48.5%) rated their skills as average in making spreadsheets in the computer. The majority of the research scholars of IIMI (60%), IITR (59%), IIML (54.28%), and IITD (49%) rated their skills highly in copying and transferring files in the computer, while postgraduate students of IIMI (67%), IIML (57.5%), IITD (55.5%) and IITR (52%) rated their skills highly. The maximum number of research scholars of IIMI (58.57%), IIML (50%), IITR (49%), and IITD (43.5%) rated their skills highly in drawing pictures whereas postgraduate students of IIML (49%), IIMI (48%), IITR (44%) and IITD (43%) rated highly in drawing pictures. In making power point presentations, the majority of the research scholars of IIML (52.85%), IITD (52%), IITR (49.5%) rated their skills highly except IIMI (55.71%) rated skills as average in making PPT while postgraduate students of IITR (57%), IIML (56.5%), and IITD (43.5%) rated their skills highly except IIMI (50.5%) who rated their skills as average.

It can be concluded that based on the above data the number of research scholars of IIML and IIMI (58.57%) rated their skills highly in printing document files, IITR (62.5%) in opening and saving files, IIMI (61.42%) in making spreadsheets,

Table 3.3.7: Computer Literacy Skills

Skills	IITD						IITR						IIML						IIMI					
	RS N=200			PGS N=200			RS N=200			PGS N=200			RS N=70			PGS N=200			RS N=70			PGS N=200		
	H	A	L	H	A	L	H	A	L	H	A	L	H	A	L	H	A	L	H	A	L	H	A	L
Print Document file	112 (56%)	75 (37.5%)	13 (6.5%)	104 (52%)	81 (40.5%)	15 (7.5%)	109 (54.5%)	71 (35.5%)	20 (10%)	102 (51%)	89 (44.5%)	9 (4.5%)	41 (58.57%)	24 (34.28%)	5 (7.15%)	114 (57%)	75 (37.5%)	11 (5.5%)	41 (58.57%)	22 (31.42%)	7 (10%)	108 (54%)	80 (40%)	12 (6%)
Open and save file	103 (51,5%)	86 (43%)	11 (5.5%)	98 (49%)	87 (43.5%)	15 (7.5%)	125 (62.5%)	71 (35.5%)	4 (2%)	129 (64.5%)	69 (34.5%)	2 (1%)	43 (61.42%)	21 (30%)	6 (8.58%)	128 (64%)	68 (34%)	4 (2%)	41 (58.57%)	23 (32.85%)	8 (4%)	121 (60.5%)	70 (35%)	9 (4.5%)
Make a spreadsheet	112 (56%)	79 (39.5%)	9 (4.5%)	88 (44%)	97 (48.5%)	15 (7.5%)	109 (54.5%)	78 (39%)	13 (6.5%)	87 (43.5%)	99 (49.5%)	14 (7%)	41 (58.58%)	21 (30%)	8 (11.42%)	79 (39.5%)	107 (53.5%)	14 (7%)	43 (61.42%)	17 (24.28%)	10 (14.30%)	81 (40.5%)	110 (55%)	9 (4.5%)
Copy/ transfer file	98 (49%)	82 (41%)	20 (10%)	111 (55.5%)	78 (39%)	11 (5.5%)	118 (59%)	71 (35.5%)	11 (5.5%)	104 (52%)	84 (42%)	12 (6%)	38 (54.28%)	19 (27.14%)	13 (18.58%)	115 (57.5%)	69 (34.5%)	16 (8%)	42 (60%)	23 (32.85%)	5 (7.15%)	134 (67%)	61 (30.5%)	5 (2.5%)
Draw picture	87(43.5%)	98 (49%)	15 (7.5%)	86 (43%)	109 (54.5%)	5 (2.5%)	98 (49%)	87 (43.5%)	15 (7.5%)	88 (44%)	91 (45.5%)	21 (10.5%)	35 (50%)	22 (31.42%)	13 (18.58%)	98 (49%)	78 (39%)	24 (12%)	41 (58.57%)	27 (38.57%)	2 (2.86%)	96 (48%)	102 (51%)	2 (1%)
Make power point presentation (PPT)	104 (52%)	88 (44%)	8 (4%)	87 (43.5%)	78 (39%)	35 (17.5%)	99 (49.5%)	83 (41.5%)	18 (9%)	114 (57%)	80 (40%)	6 (3%)	37 (52.85%	22 (31.42%)	11 (15.71%)	112 (56%)	79 (39.5%)	9 (4.5%)	26 (37.15%)	39 (55.71%)	5 (7.14%)	88 (44%)	101 (50.5%)	11(5,5%)
Mean	102.67	84.67	12.67	95.67	88.33	16.00	109.67	76.83	13.50	104.00	85.33	10.67	39.17	21.50	9.33	107.67	79.33	13.00	39.00	25.17	6.17	104.67	87.33	8.00
SD	9.42	8.04	4.41	10.37	12.42	10.10	10.54	7.00	5.68	15.96	10.29	6.62	2.99	1.64	3.50	16.98	14.29	6.81	6.42	7.49	2.79	20.26	19.82	3.79

H=High, A=Average, L=Low

IIMI (60%) in copying and transferring files, IIMI (58.57%) in drawing pictures rated their skills highly except for power point presentations rated their skills as average, whereas postgraduate students of IIMI (54%), IITR (64.5%), IIMI (67%), IIML (49%) rated their skills highly in printing document files, opening and saving files, copying and transferring files and picture drawing. The majority of postgraduate students of IIML (58.58%) and IIMI (55%), IITR (49.5%) and IITD (48.5%) rated their skill average in spreadsheet making and IIMI (50.5%) rated their skills as average in Power Point presentations.

Statistical Inference

Majority of RS and PG students of IITD, IITR, IIML and IIMI rated their skills highly in make a spreadsheet.

Table 3.3.8: Familiarity with Social Media Platform

Social Media Platforms	IITD		IITR		IIML		IIMI	
	RS N=200	PGS N=200	RS N=200	PGS N=200	RS N=70	PGS N=200	RS N=70	PGS N=200
Facebook	134 (67%)	141 (70.5%)	113 (56.5%)	139 (69.5%)	43 (61.42%)	87 (43.5%)	49 (70%)	97 (48.5%)
Twitter	97 (48.5%)	76 (38%)	82 (41%)	55 (27.5%)	32 (45.71%)	75 (37.5%)	41 (58.6%)	72 (36%)
What Apps	145 (72.5%)	123 (61.5%)	135 (67.5%)	161 (80.5%)	52 (74.28%)	132 (66%)	55 (78.6%)	121 (60.5%)
Orkut	87 (43.5%)	57 (28.5%)	69 (34.5%)	48 (24%)	21 (30%)	78 (39%)	7 (10%)	15 (7.5%)
Blogs	145 (72.5%)	102 (51%)	99 (49.5%)	96 (48%)	45 (64.28%)	98 (49%)	36 (51.4%)	124 (62%)
Worldflot	57 (28.5%)	21 (10.5%)	13 (6.5%)	0	1 (1.42%)	15 (7.5%)	0	3 (1.5%)
Any other	0	2 (1%)	0	2 (1%)	0	0	0	0
Mean	95.00	74.57	73.00	71.57	27.71	69.29	26.86	61.71
SD	53.32	51.57	50.24	63.16	21.08	46.42	23.81	55.05

(Multiple Answers permitted)

Social media is fast becoming a regular part of libraries. Its presents many opportunities for libraries, and is reasonably well embedded in library communications. Social media is moving towards a central role in how libraries are communicating with their end users. Table 4.3.8 depicts that among research scholars of IIMI i.e. 49 (70%), 134 (67%) of IITD, 43, 61.42% of IIML and 113 (56.5%) of IITR used Facebook as their social media platform, whereas postgraduate students of IITD, i.e. 141 (70.5%), 139 (69.5%) of IITR, 97 (48.5%) of IIMI and 87 (43.5%) of IIMI. Most of the research scholars of IITD i.e. 97 (48.5%), 82 (41%) of IITR, 41 (58.57%) of IIMI and 75 (37.5%) of IIML used Twitter as their social media platform, while postgraduate students of IITR, i.e. 76 (38%), 75 (37.5%) of IIML, 72 (36%) of IIMI and 55 (27.5%) of IITR. Majority of the research scholars of IIMI i.e. 55 (78.57%), 52 (74.28%) of IIML, 145 (72.5%) of IITD, 135 (67.5%) of IITR used WhatsApp as a social media platform for their services, whereas postgraduate students of IITR, i.e. 161(80.5%), 132 (66%) of IIML, 123 (61.5%) of IITD, and 121 (60.5%) of IIMI used WhatsApp for their services. The majority of the research scholars of IITD, i.e. 145 (72.5%), 45 (64.28%) of IIML, 36 (51.24%) of IIMI, and 99 (49.5%) of IITR used Blogs as a social media platform, while postgraduate students of IIMI, i.e. 124 (62%), 102 (51%) of IITD, 98 (49%) of IIML and 96 (48%) of IITR used Blogs as a social media platform. All these responses indicate that postgraduate students were more familiar with Facebook, and WhatsApp than the research scholars. Thus, they were able to make use of these social media platforms for their services.

Statistical Inference

Research scholars of institutions prefer What Apps as a social media platforms. IIMI RS response uses more (78.6%), IIML RS (74.28%), IITD RS (72.5%) and IITTR (58.57%). Trend of IIMs PG students uses of What Apps as a social media platforms is slightly more, IITR PG students (80.5%), (66%) in IIML, (61.5%) IITD and (60.5%) IIMI.

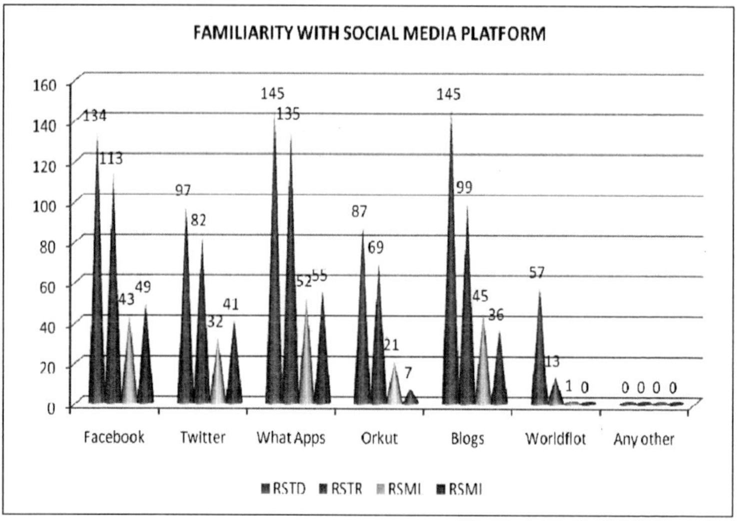

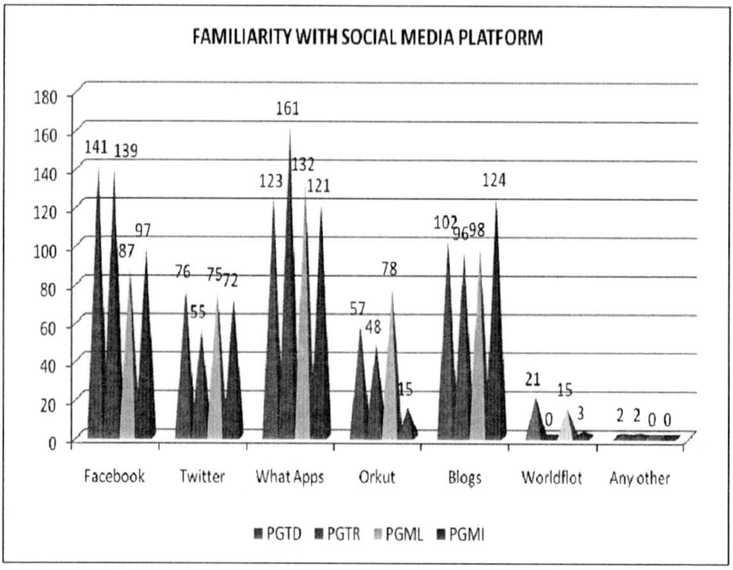

Table 3.3.9 indicates that the majority of the research scholars of IIML, i.e. 53 (75.71%) more than IIMI 44 (62.85%), IITD 102 (51%), and IITR 81 (40.5%) used Google Chrome, while

Table 3.3.9: Familiarity with Internet Browser

Internet Browser	IITD		IITR		IIML		IIMI	
	RS N=200	PGS N=200	RS N=200	PGS N=200	RS N=70	PGS N=200	RS N=70	PGS N=200
Google Chrome	102 (51%)	97 (48.5%)	81 (40.5%)	113 (56.5%)	53 (75.71%)	132 (66%)	44 (62.85%)	94 (47%)
Mozilla Firefox	86 (43%)	107 (53.5%)	58 (29%)	92 (46%)	32 (45.71%)	54 (27%)	39 (55.71%)	81 (40.5%)
Internet Explorer	78 (39%)	87 (43.5%)	54 (27%)	82 (41%)	26 (37.14%)	83 (41.5%)	41 (58.57%)	72 (36%)
Opera	45 (22.5%)	8 (4%)	7 (3.5%)	18 (9%)	5 (7.14%)	31 (15.5%)	6 (8.57%)	6 (3.5%)
Any other	-	-	-	-	-	-	-	-
Mean	62.20	59.80	40.00	61.00	23.20	60.00	26.00	50.60
SD	40.51	51.50	34.96	49.18	21.46	50.47	21.18	44.20

(Multiple Answers permitted)

postgraduate students of IIML, i.e. 132 (66%), IITR 113 (56.5%), IITD 97 (48.5%), and IIMI 94 (47%) used Google Chrome as Internet Browser. The maximum number of research scholars of IIMI, i.e. 39 (55.71%) more than IIML 32 (45.71%), IITD 86 (43%) and IITR 58 (29%) used Mozilla Firefox, while postgraduate student of IITD 107 (53.5%) more than IITR 92 (46%), IIMI 81 (40.5%) and IIML 54 (27%) used Mozilla Firefox as a browser. Most of the research scholars of IIMI, i.e. 41 (58.57%) more than IITD 78 (39%), IIML 26 (37.14%), and IITR 54 (27%) used Internet Explorer as a browser, while postgraduate students of IITD, i.e. 87 (43.5%) more than IIML 83 (41.5%), IITR 82 (41%) and IIMI 72 (36%) used Internet Explorer.

It can be concluded from this table that Google Chrome was more used as browser 38 (54.28%), while the least used browser was Opera 5 (2.5%).

Statistical Inference

Table number 3.3.9 shows that the maximum responses of RS and PG Students of institutions received for the option FAMILIARITY WITH INTERNET BROWSER is "Google Chrome". RS responses are as IIML (75.71%), IITD (51%), IIMI (62.85%), IITR (40.5%) and responses of PG students are (66%), (56.5%), (48.5%), (47%) of IIML, IITR, IITD and IIMI

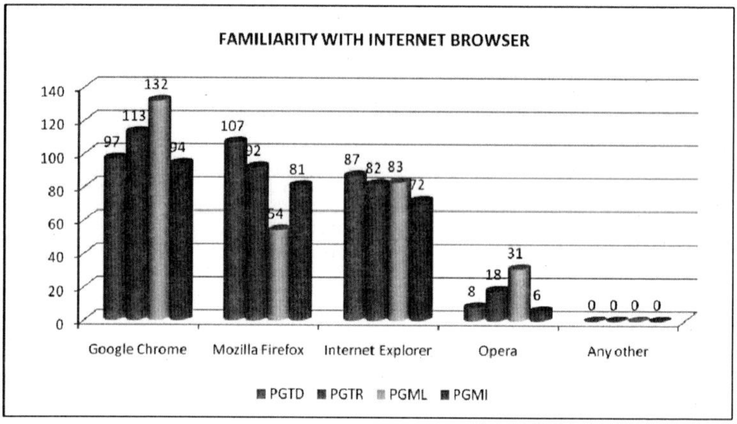

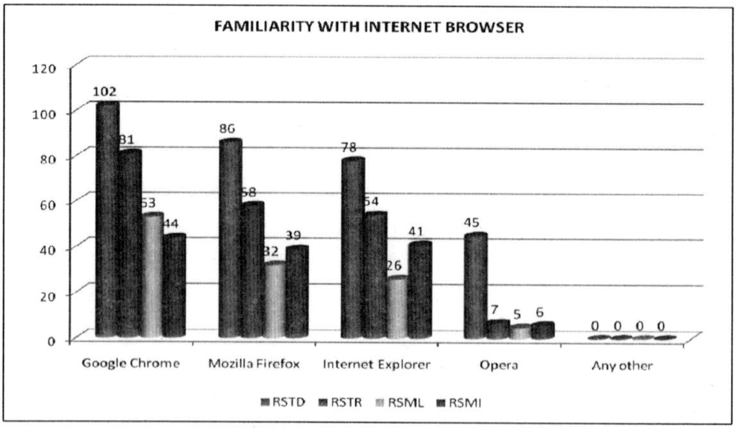

respectively. Furthermore, a similarity seen in the least percentage of responses received for Opera.

Table 3.3.10: Familiarity with Search Engines

Search Engines	IITD		IITR		IIML		IIMI	
	RS N=200	PGS N=200	RS N=200	PGS N=200	RS N=70	PGS N=200	RS N=70	PGS N=200
Google	143 (71.5%)	133 (66.5%)	123 (61.5%)	156 (78%)	48 (68.57%)	159 (79.5%)	57 (81.42%)	144 (72%)
Yahoo	112 (56%)	97 (48.5%)	115 (57.5%)	123 (61.5%)	39 (55.71%)	141 (70.5%)	37 (52.85%)	98 (49%)
Rediff	82 (41%)	53 (26.5%)	75 (37.5%)	53 (26.5%)	29 (41.42%)	63 (31.5%)	31 (15.5%)	65 (32.5%)
Bing	39 (19.5%)	24 (12%)	41 (20.5%)	37 (18.5%)	22 (31.42%)	27 (13.5%)	24 (12%)	23 (11.5%)
Lycos	11 (5.5%)	6 (3%)	3 (1.5%)	7 (3.5%)	9 (12.85%)	12 (6%)	-	2 (1%)
Any other	-	-	-	-	-	-	-	
Mean	64.50	52.17	59.50	62.67	24.50	67.00	24.83	55.33
SD	57.27	53.27	53.72	63.45	18.05	67.93	22.16	57.84

(Multiple Answers permitted)

Table 3.3.10 shows that search engines were frequently used by the research scholars and postgraduate students of selected libraries. The majority of the research scholars of IIMI, i.e. 57 (81.42%) more than IITD 143 (71.5%), IIML 48 (68.57%) and IITR 123 (61.5%) used Google search engines, while postgraduate students of IIML 159 (79.5%) more than IITR 156 (78%), IIMI 144 (72%) and IITD 133 (66.5%) used Google. The maximum number of research scholars of IITR i.e. 115 (57.5%) more than IITD 112 (56%), IIML 39 (55.71%) and IIMI 37 (52.85%) used Yahoo search engine, while postgraduate students of IIML 141(70.5%) more than IITR 123 (61.5%), IIMI 98 (49%) and IITD 97 (48.5%) used Yahoo search engine. Bing search engine was used more by the research scholars of IIML 22 (31.42%) than postgraduate students.

Statistical Inference

Table number 3.3.10 shows that the maximum responses of RS and PG Students of institutions received for the option

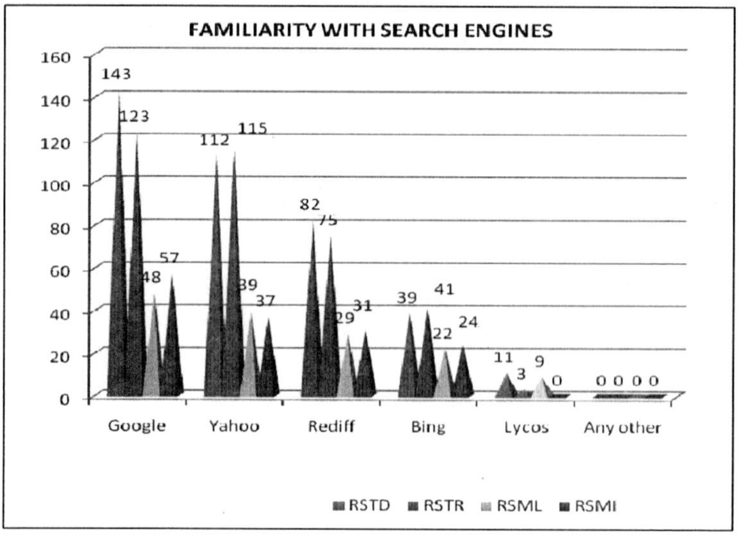

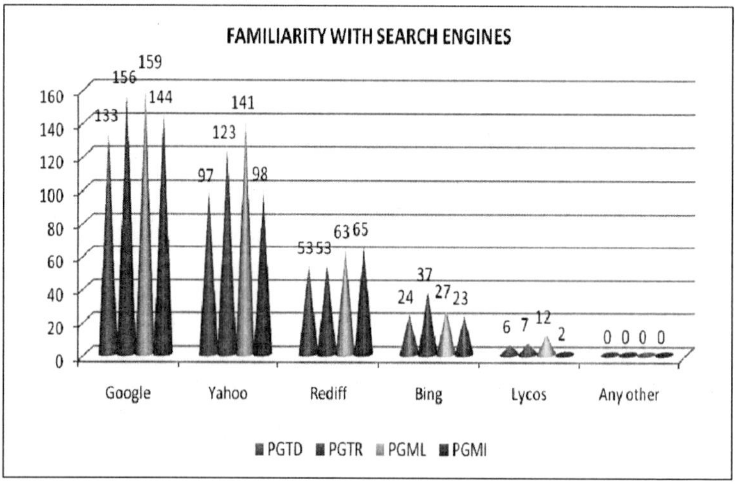

familiarity with search engines is "Google". RS responses are as IIMI (81.42%), IITD (71.5%), IITR (61.5%), IIML (68.57%) and responses of PG students are (79.5%), (78%), (72%), (66.5%) of IIML, IITR, IIMI and IITD respectively. Furthermore, a similarity seen in the least percentage of responses received for Lycos.

Table 3.3.11: Tools for Locating Documents on Shelves

Options	IITD		IITR		IIML		IIMI	
	RS N=200	PGS N=200	RS N=200	PGS N=200	RS N=70	PGS N=200	RS N=70	PGS N=200
Call Number	38 (19%)	28 (14%)	41 (20.5%)	27 (13.5%)	31 (44.28%)	29 (14.5%)	25 (35.71%)	61 (30.5%)
Title	63 (31.5%)	56 (28%)	47 (23.5%)	49 (24.5%)	12 (17.14%)	44 (22%)	18 (25.73%)	41 (20.5%)
Author	39 (19.5%)	49 (24.5%)	55 (27.5%)	65 (32.5%)	9 (12.85%)	62 (31%)	8 (11.42%)	31 (15.5%)
Subject	60 (30%)	67 (33.5%)	57 (28.5%)	59 (29.5%)	18 (25.73%)	65 (32.5%)	19 (27.14%)	67 (33.5%)
Total	200 (100%)	200 (100%)	200 (100%)	200 (100%)	70 (100%)	200 (100%)	70 (100%)	200 (100%)
Mean	50.00	50.00	50.00	50.00	17.50	50.00	17.50	50.00
SD	13.34	16.43	7.39	16.69	9.75	16.79	7.05	16.85

To identify the respondents' awareness with the call number, they were asked what was needed to find a document on the shelves in the library. Table 3.3.11 shows that among research scholars, 31 (44.28%) of IIML, 25 (35.71%) of IIMI, 41 (20.5%) of IITR and 38 (19%) of IITD prefer the correct option 'call number. Among the postgraduate students, 61 (30.5%) of IIMI, 29 (14.5%) of IIML, 28 (14%) of IITD and 27 (13.5%) of IITR prefer the right option.

It is clear from the table that all these responses indicate that research scholars and postgraduate students of IIMI and IIML were more familiar with the call number for locating documents on the shelves than the research scholars and postgraduate students of IITR and IITD. Most of the postgraduate students, 67 (33.5%) of IITD and IIMI, 65 (32.5%) of IIML, 59 (29.5%) of IITR indicated that they searched for books according to the subject of the book while research scholars, 60 (30%) of IITD, 57 (28.5%) IITR, 19 (27.14%) of IIMI and 18 (25.73%) searched for books according to the subject of the books.

Statistical inference

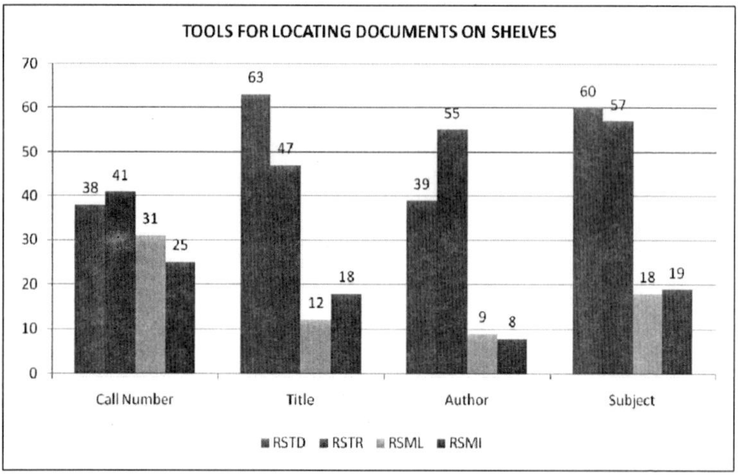

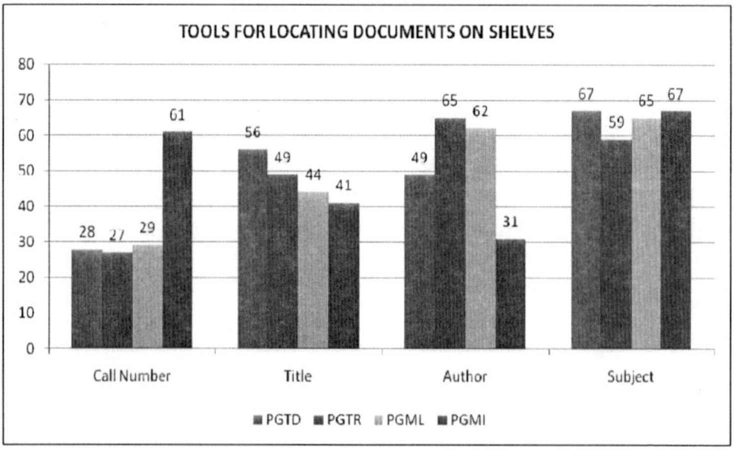

Table 3.3.11 shows that only RS of IITD (31.5%) prefer "Title" for locating documents on shelves, in contrast RS of IITR (28.5%) prefer "Subject" and RS of IIMs prefer "Call number" with (44.28%), (35.71%) IIML, IIMI respectively.

In PGS responses, trend is in contrast. None of institutions PGS prefer "Title". The responses of PGS institutions prefer "Subject" with (33.5%), 29.5%), (32.5%) and (33.5%) of IITD, IITR, IIML and IIMI respectively.

Table 3.3.12: Awareness of Search Techniques and Srategies

Search Techniques and Strategies	IITD		IITR		IIML		IIMI	
	RS N=200	PGS N=200	RS N=200	PGS N=200	RS N=70	PGS N=200	RS N=70	PGS N=200
Simple Keywords	54 (27%)	77 (38.5%)	45 (22.5%)	69 (34.5%)	33 (47.14%)	74 (37%)	26 (37.14%)	69 (34.5%)
Boolean Operators (AND, OR, NOT)	21 (10.5%)	25 (12.5%)	35 (17.5%)	33 (16.5%)	12 (17.14%)	20 (10%)	8 (11.42%)	29 (14.5%)
Truncation	43 (21.5%)	34 (17%)	31 (15.5%)	36 (18%)	8 (11.44%)	20 (10%)	7 (10%)	17 (8.5%)
Field Search (title, author, subject, etc.)	82 (41%)	64 (32%)	89 (44.5%)	62 (31%)	17 (24.28%)	86 (43%)	29 (41.44%)	85 (42.5%)
Total	200 (100%)	200 (100%)	200 (100%)	200 (100%)	70 (100%)	200 (100%)	70 (100%)	200 (100%)
Mean	50.00	50.00	50.00	50.00	17.50	50.00	17.50	50.00
SD	25.36	24.54	26.66	18.17	10.97	34.99	11.62	32.23

Table 3.3.12 depicts that the majority of research scholars of IIML i.e. 33 (47.14%), 69 (34.5%) of IIMI, 54 (27%) of IITD and 45 (22.5%) of IITR used simple keywords search, while postgraduate students of IITD, i.e. 77 (38.5%), 74 (37%) of IIML, 69 (34.5%) of IIMI and IITD used simple keywords search. The majority of the research scholars of IITR, i.e. 35 (17.5%), 12 (17.14%) of IIML, 8 (11.42%) of IIMI, and 21 (10.5%) of IITD

used Boolean operators, while postgraduate students of IITR i.e. 33 (16.5%), 29 (14.5%) of IIMI, 25 (12.5%) of IITD and 20 (10%) of IIML used Boolean operators for searching documents. The number of research scholars of IITR, i.e. 89 (44.5%), 29 (41.44%) of IIMI, 82 (41%) of IITD and 17 (24.28%) of IIML used field search (title, author, subject, etc) while postgraduate students of IIML, i.e. 86 (43%), 85 (42.5%) of IIMI, 64 (32%) of IITD, 61 (31%) of IIT, Roorkee used field search for searching documents. It can be inferred from the data that the field search (title, author, subject, etc.) were used more by the research scholars and postgraduate students than simple search, and Boolean operators were used less by research scholars and postgraduate students for searching documents.

Statistical Inference

The highest number of RS responses was obtained for Field Search in IITR (44.5%), IIMI (41.44%) , IITD (41%) in contrast RS of IIML (47.14%) responses were obtained for Simple Keywords.

Responses of PGS of all institutes were obtained in reverse of RS responses. PGS responses IITs was obtained for Simple Keywords. IITD (38.5%), IITR (34.5%) in contrast PGS responses of IIMs for Field Search. IIML (43%) and IIMI (42.5%).

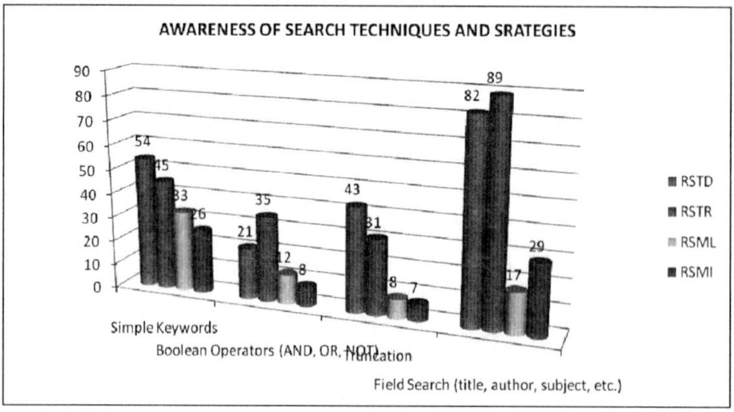

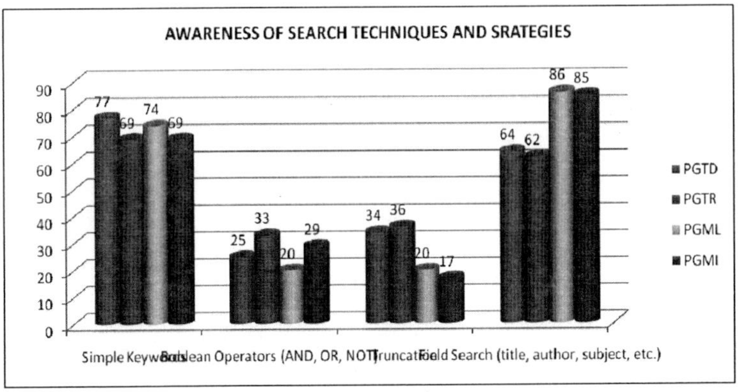

Table 3.3.13 indicates the level of internet literacy skills of the research scholars and postgraduate students of the selected libraries, i.e. IITD, IITR, IIML and IIMI. Most of the research scholars of IIML 48 (68.57%) rated their skills highly to write and send e-mails than IIMI 45 (64.28%), IITD 113 (56.5%) and IITR 92 (46%), while the majority of the postgraduate students of IIMI 116 (58%) rated their skills more highly than IITR 111 (55.5%), IITD 103 (51.5%), IIML 98 (37%) in writing and sending e-mails. The majority of the research scholars of IITR 88 (44%) rated their skills as average to write and send e-mails than IITD 87 (43.5%), IIML 22 (31.43%), and IIMI 19 (27.14%), whereas postgraduate students of IIML 87 (43.5%) rated their skills average more than IITD 85 (42.5%), IIMI 74 (37%), and IITR 67 (33.5%) in writing and sending email. To attach files to an e-mail, the majority of research scholars of IIMI 46 (65.74%) rated their skills more highly than IIML 43 (61.42%), IITD 45 (57.5%) and IITR 107 (53.5%) while postgraduate students of IIML 102 (51%) more than IIMI 98 (49%), IITD 97 (48.5%) and IITR 71 (35.5%) rated their skills highly in attaching files to an e-mail. Most of the research scholars of IITR 86 (43%) rated their skills as average in attaching files to an email more than IITD 76 (38%), IIML 25 (35.71%) and IIMI 23 (32.85%) while postgraduate students of IITD 85 (42.5%), IIML 82 (41%), and IITR and IIMI 71 (35.5%) rated their skills as average in attaching files to an email. The majority of the research scholars

Table 3.3.13: Internet Literacy Skills

SD	Mean	Search in Web OPAC	Download scholarly article	Copy/ download files	Web browsing	Attach a file to an e-mail	Write and send e-mail	Skills		
21.09	95.83	57 (28.5%)	91 (45.5%)	98 (49%)	101 (50.5%)	115 (57.5%)	113 (56.5%)	H	RS N=200	IITD
7.48	82.50	89 (44.5%)	71 (35.5%)	89 (44.5%)	83 (41.5%)	76 (38%)	87 (43.5%)	A		
20.25	21.67	54 (27%)	38 (19%)	13 (6.5%)	16 (8%)	9 (4.5%)	0 (0%)	L		
19.49	85.83	48 (24%)	89 (44.5%)	92 (46%)	86 (43%)	97 (48.5%)	103 (51.5%)	H	PGS N=200	
13.59	86.00	61 (30.5%)	92 (46%)	101 (50.5%)	92 (46%)	85 (42.5%)	85 (42.5%)	A		
31.79	33.00	91 (45.5%)	48 (24%)	7 (3.5%)	22 (11%)	18 (9%)	12 (6%)	L		
16.13	95.50	66 (33%)	97 (48.5%)	112 (56%)	99 (49.5%)	107 (53.5%)	92 (46%)	H	RS N=200	IITR
3.27	84.50	81 (40.5%)	88 (44%)	83 (41.5%)	81 (40.5%)	86 (43%)	88 (44%)	A		
17.37	20.00	53 (26.5%)	15 (7.5%)	5 (2.5%)	20 (10%)	7 (3.5%)	20 (10%)	L		
19.85	82.67	49 (24.5%)	84 (42%)	83 (41.5%)	81 (40.5%)	88 (44%)	111 (55.5%)	H	PGS N=200	
17.10	79.50	56 (28%)	93 (46.5%)	98 (49%)	92 (46%)	71 (35.5%)	67 (33.5%)	A		
29.05	37.83	95 (47.5%)	23 (11.5%)	19 (9.5%)	27 (13.5%)	41 (20.5%)	22 (11%)	L		
5.91	39.83	31 (44.28%)	36 (51.42%)	39 (55.72%)	42 (60%)	43 (61.42%)	48 (68.57%)	H	RS N=70	IIML
2.07	25.50	25 (35.72%)	27 (38.57%)	26 (37.14%)	28 (40%)	25 (35.71%)	22 (31.43%)	A		
5.35	4.67	14 (20%)	7 (10%)	5 (7.14%)	0 (0%)	2 (2.85%)	0 (0%)	L		
18.88	83.17	49 (24.5%)	83 (41.5%)	88 (44%)	79 (39.5%)	102 (51%)	98 (49%)	H	PGS N=200	
14.62	80.83	61 (30.5%)	67 (33.5%)	101 (50.5%)	87 (43.5%)	82 (41%)	87 (43.5%)	A		
32.02	40.00	90 (45%)	50 (25%)	11 (5.5%)	34 (17%)	16 8%)	15 (7.5%)	L		
6.18	39.83	30 (42.85%)	35 (50%)	41 (58.57%)	42 (60%)	46 (65.74%)	45 (64.28%)	H	RS N=70	IIMI
2.94	20.67	17 (24.28%)	19 (27.14%)	25 (35.71%)	21 (30%)	23 (32.85%)	19 (27.14%)	A		
8.31	9.50	23 (32.85%)	16 (22.86%)	4 (5.72%)	7 (10%)	1 (1.41%)	6 (8.58%)	L		
22.87	81.67	51 (25.5%)	71 (35.5%)	71 (35.5%)	83 (41.5%)	98 (49%)	116 (58%)	H	PGS N=200	
16.22	82.67	62 (31%)	88 (44%)	98 (49%)	103 (51.5%)	71 (35.5%)	74 (37%)	A		
21.09	95.83	87 (43.5%)	41 (20.5%)	31 (15.5%)	14 (7%)	31 (15.5%)	10 (5%)	L		

H=High, A=Average, L=Low

of IIML and IIMI 42 (60%) rated their skills highly in web browsing than IITD 101 (50.5%) and IITR 99 (49.5%) while postgraduate students of IITD 86 (43%) more than IIMI 83 (41.5%), IITR 81 (40.5%) and IIML 79 (39.5%) in web browsing. The number of research scholars of IITD 89 (44.5%) rated their skills as average than IITR 83 (41.5%), IIML 26 (37.14%) and IIMI 25 (35.71%) in copying and downloading files while postgraduate students of IITD and IIML 101 (50.5%) more than IITR and IIMI 98 (49%) rated their skills as average. In downloading scholarly articles, the majority of the research scholars of IIML 36 (51.42%) rated their skills more highly than IIMI 35 (50%), IITR 97 (48.5%) and IITD 91 (45.5%), while postgraduate students of IITD 89 (44.5%), IITR 84 (42%), IIML 83 (41.5%) and IIMI 71 (35.5%) rated their skills highly in downloading scholarly articles.

These findings suggest that the research scholars of IITR 88 (44%) rated their skills as average than IIML 27 (38.57%), IITD 71 (35.5%) and IIMI 19 (27.4%) while postgraduate students of IITR 93 (46.5%) more than IITD 92 (46%), IIMI 88 (44%) and IIML 67 (33.5%) rated their skills as average in downloading scholarly articles. The number of research scholars of IIML 31 (44.28%) and IIMI 30 (42.85%) rated their skills highly for searching in Web OPAC while that majority of postgraduate student of IITR 95 (47.5%), IITD 91 (45.5%), IIML 90 (45%) and IIMI 87 (43.5%) rated themselves as low. Most of the research scholars of IITD 89 (44.5%) and IITR 81 (40.5%) rated their skills as average for searching in Web OPAC.

Table 3.3.14 represents that the research scholars of IIML 16 (22.86%), IITD 44 (22%), IIMI 12 (17.14%) and IITR 31 (15.5%) are aware of information literacy standards/guidelines/policies and postgraduate students of IIML 58 (29%), IIMI 41 (20.5%), IITD 29 (14.5%), and IITR 19 (9.5%) were aware of information literacy standards, guidelines and policies. The number of research scholars of IITR 169 (84.5%), IIMI 58 (82.86%), IITD 156 (78%) and IIML 54 (77.14%) do not have a proper understanding of information literacy standards/

Table 3.3.14:
Awareness of Information Literacy Standards/ Guidelines/Policies

Response	IITD		IITR		IIML		IIMI	
	RS N=200	PGS N=200	RS N=200	PGS N=200	RS N=70	PGS N=200	RS N=70	PGS N=200
Yes	44 (22%)	29 (14.5%)	31 (15.5%)	19 (9.5%)	16 (22.86%)	58 (29%)	12 (17.14%)	41 (20.5%)
No	156 (78%)	171 (85.5%)	169 (84.5%)	181 (90.5%)	54 (77.14%)	142 (71%)	58 (82.86%)	159 (79.5%)
Total	200 (100%)	200 (100%)	200 (100%)	200 (100%)	70 (100%)	200 (100%)	70 (100%)	200 (100%)
Mean	100.00	100.00	100.00	100.00	35.00	100.00	35.00	100.00
SD	79.20	100.41	97.58	114.55	26.87	59.40	32.53	83.44

guidelines/policies and postgraduate students of IITR 181 (90.5%), IITD 171 (85.5%), IIMI 159 (79.5%), and IIML 142 (71%) are also not aware of information literacy standards, guidelines and policies.

Statistical Inference

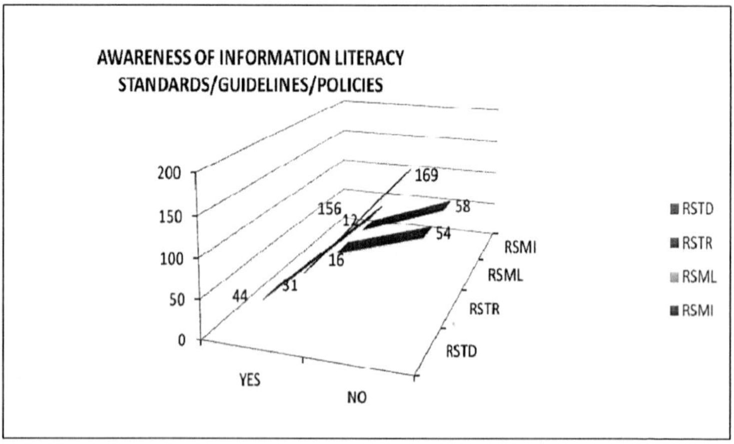

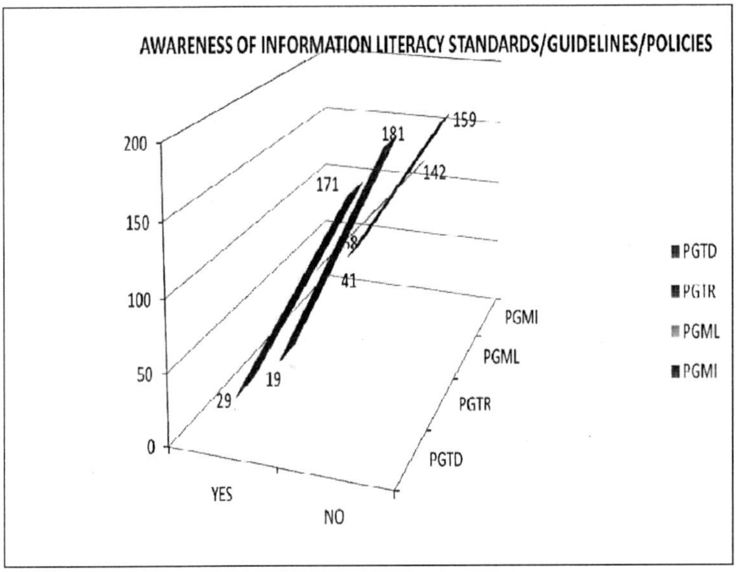

It is visible from the table that RS and PGS responses 'YES' was minimum percentage of awareness of information literacy standards/guidelines/policies.

Table 3.3.15 shows the frequency of information literacy programmes which were organized by the selected libraries, i.e. IITD, IITR, IIML and IIMI. The majority of the research scholars of IIML 51 (72.85%), 43 (61.42%) of IIMI, 85 (42.5%) of IITD, 84 (42%) of IITR participated at the starting of the academic year in information literacy programmes, while postgraduate students of IIML, i.e. 71 (35.5%), IITD 67 (33.5%), IIMI 66 (33%), IITR 65 (32.5%) were participated. Somewhere in the middle of the Courses, majority of the research scholars of IITD, i.e. 65 (32.5%), IITR 41 (20.5%), IIMI 7 (10%) and IIML 5 (7.14%) participated in information literacy programmes while postgraduate students of IITR 54 (27%), IITD and IIML 52 (26%) participated in ILP. The number of research scholars of IITR 62 (31%), shown that no fixed time for participating in information literacy programmes than IIMI 20 (28.58%), IITD 39 (19.5%), IIML 12 (17.14%) while postgraduate students of

Table 3.3.15: Frequency of Information Literacy Programmes

Frequency	IITD		IITR		IIML		IIMI	
	RS N=200	PGS N=200	RS N=200	PGS N=200	RS N=70	PGS N=200	RS N=70	PGS N=200
Starting of the academic year	85 (42.5%)	67 (33.5%)	84 (42%)	65 (32.5%)	51 (72.85%)	71 (35.5%)	43 (61.42%)	66 (33%)
Monthly basis	11 (5.5%)	8 (4%)	13 (6.5%)	6 (3%)	2 (2.87%)	4 (2%)	-	3 (1.5%)
Somewhere in the middle of the course	65 (32.5%)	52 (26%)	41 (20.5%)	54 (27%)	5 (7.14%)	52 (26%)	7 (10%)	35 (17.5%)
No fixed time	39 (19.5%)	73 (36.5%)	62 (31%)	75 (37.5%)	12 (17.14%)	73 (36.5%)	20 (28.58%)	96 (48%)
Total	200 (100%)	200 (100%)	200 (100%)	200 (100%)	70 (100%)	200 (100%)	70 (100%)	200 (100%)
Mean	50.00	50.00	50.00	50.00	17.50	50.00	17.50	50.00
SD	32.10	29.36	30.28	30.56	22.72	32.09	18.91	40.02

IIMI 96 (48%) more than IITR 75 (37.5%), IITD and IIML 62 (31%) had no fixed time for participating in ILP.

Statistical Inference

Table 3.3.15 mean score shows that, the highest number of responses above the mean were obtained for "Starting of the academic year" and the lowest number of responses were observed in case of "Monthly basis" closest to the mean score were the number of responses that were obtained from the RS and PGS who said " Some Where in the middle". While, the mean score received for RS and PGS, IITD (RS) (Mean=50.0, SD=32.10), IITD (PGS) (Mean=50.0, SD=29.36), IITR (RS)

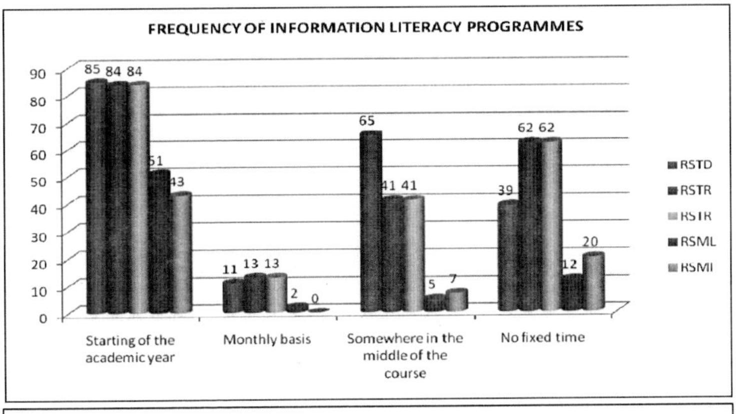

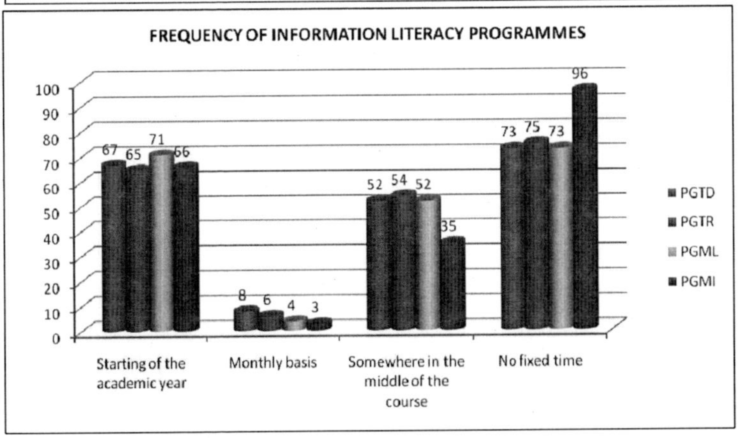

(Mean=50.0, SD=30.28), IITR (PGS) (Mean=50.0, SD=30.56), IIML (RS) (Mean=17.50, SD=22.72), IIML (PGS) (Mean=50.0, SD= 32.09), IIMI (RS) (Mean=17.50, SD=18.91), IIMI (PGS) (Mean=50.0, SD=40.02)

Table 3.3.16:
Responsible for Conducting Information Literacy Programme

Responsible for conducting of ILP	IITD		IITR		IIML		IIMI	
	RS N=200	PGS N=200	RS N=200	PGS N=200	RS N=70	PGS N=200	RS N=70	PGS N=200
Librarian	118 (59%)	98 (49%)	114 (57%)	116 (58%)	37 (52.85%)	110 (55%)	41 (58.57%)	112 (56%)
Other library staff	8 (4%)	13 (6.5%)	5 (2.5%)	9 (4.5%)	6 (8.57%)	12 (6%)	5 (7.14%)	11 (5.5%)
Faculty	14 (7%)	12 (6%)	16 (8%)	20 (10%)	12 (17.14%)	9 (4.5%)	7 (10%)	13 (6.5%)
Both librarian and faculty	36 (18%)	55 (27.5%)	46 (23%)	43 (21.5%)	13 (18.57%)	54 (27%)	5 (7.14%)	54 (27%)
Staff of E-publishers	24 (12%)	22 (11%)	19 (9.5%)	12 (6%)	2 (2.87%)	15 (7.5%)	12 (17.15%	10 (5%)
Mean	40.00	40.00	40.00	27.00	27.00	27.00	27.00	40.00
SD	44.88	36.83	44.03	44.53	13.62	43.20	15.36	44.30

The table depicts that the librarians were mainly responsible for conducting information literacy programmes. It is found from Table 3.3.16 that the 118 (59%) of research scholars and 98 (49%) of postgraduate students of IITD, whereas the librarian takes responsibility for delivering information literacy programmes. On the other hand, 46 (23%) of research scholars of IITR and 55 (27.5%) of postgraduate students of IITD, where, both librarian and faculty are responsible for conducting information literacy programmes in their library.

Statistical Inference

Table 3.3.16 mean score shows that, the highest number of responses above the mean were obtained Librarian for "responsible for conducting information literacy programme"

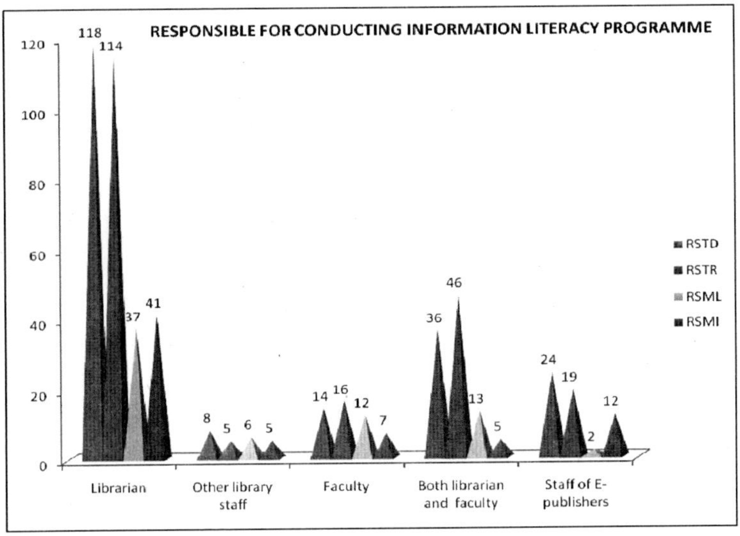

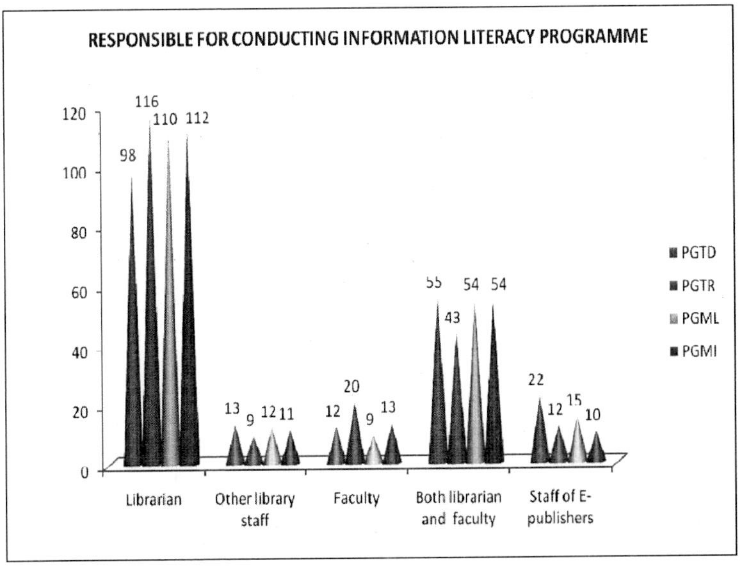

and the lowest number of responses were observed in case of "other library staff" closet to the mean score were the number of responses that were obtained from the RS and PGS who said " Both librarian and faculty". While, the mean score received for RS and PGS, IITD (RS) (Mean=40.0, SD=44.10), IITD (PGS) (Mean=40.0, SD=36.83), IITR (RS) (Mean=40.0, SD=44.03), IITR (PGS) (Mean=27.0, SD=44.53), IIML (RS) (Mean=27.50, SD=13.62), IIML (PGS) (Mean=27.0, SD= 43.20), IIMI (RS) (Mean=27.00, SD=15.36), IIMI (PGS) (Mean=40.0, SD=43.30)

Table 3.3.17: Information Literacy Programmes Attended

Response	IITD		IITR		IIML		IIMI	
	RS N=200	PGS N=200	RS N=200	PGS N=200	RS N=70	PGS N=200	RS N=70	PGS N=200
Yes	134 (67%)	145 (72.5%)	156 (78%)	137 (68.5%)	47 (67.14%)	147 (73.5%)	45 (64.28%)	134 (67%)
No	66 (33%)	55 (27.5%)	44 (22%)	63 (31.5%)	23 (32.86%)	53 (26.5%)	25 (35.72%)	66 (33%)
Mean	100.00	100.00	100.00	100.00	35.00	100.00	35.00	100.00
SD	48.08	63.64	79.20	52.33	16.97	66.47	14.14	48.08

Table 3.3.17 to know the respondents' status with attending the information literacy programme (ILP), they have been asked to mention whether they have attended the information literacy programme organized by their library or not. Table 4.3.17 shows that the majority of the research scholars of IITR 156 (78%), IIML 47 (67.14%), IITD 134 (67%), and IIMI 45 (64.28%) attended information literacy programmes while postgraduate students of IIML 147 (73.5%), ITD (145 (72.5%), IITR 137 (68.5%) and IIMI 134 (67%) attended information literacy programmes. It is found from the study that research scholars of IIMI 25 (35.72%), IITD 66 (33%), IIML 23 (32.86%) and IITR 44 (22%) did not attend information literacy programmes while postgraduate students of IIMI 66 (33%), IITR 63 (31.5%), IITD 55 (27.5%) and IIML 53 (26.5%) did not attend the information literacy programmes.

Statistical Inference

Table 3.3.17 means score shows that, the highest number of responses above the mean were "information literacy programmes attended". While, the mean score received for RS and PGS, IITD (RS) (Mean=100.0, SD=48.08), IITD (PGS) (Mean=100.0, SD=63.64), IITR (RS) (Mean=100.0, SD=79.20),

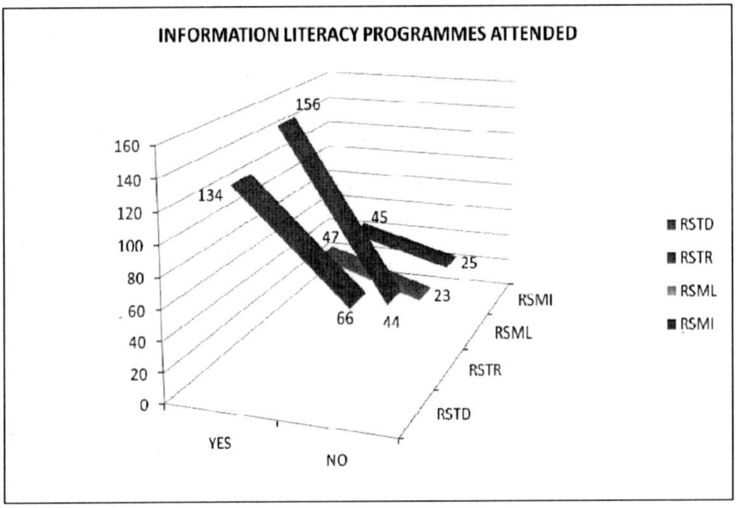

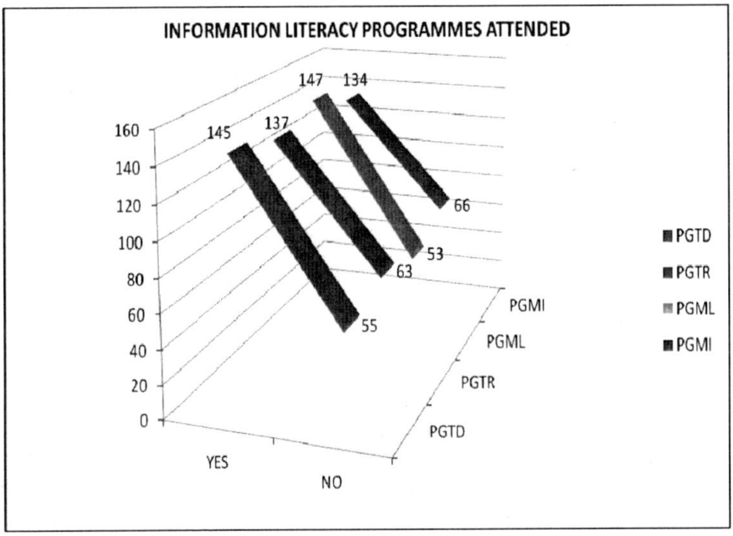

IITR (PGS) (Mean=100.0, SD=52.33), IIML (RS) (Mean=35.00, SD=16.97), IIML (PGS) (Mean=100.0, SD= 66.47), IIMI (RS) (Mean=35.00, SD=14.14), IIMI (PGS) (Mean=100.0, SD=48.08)

Table 3.3.18: Criteria used for Evaluating Information

Criteria	IITD		IITR		IIML		IIMI	
	RS N=200	PGS N=200	RS N=200	PGS N=200	RS N=70	PGS N=200	RS N=70	PGS N=200
Accuracy	115 (57.5%)	99 (49.5%)	141 (70.5%)	133 (66.5%)	43 (61.42%)	107 (53.5%)	41 (58.57%)	122 (61%)
Relevancy	121 (60.5%)	103 (51.5%)	134 (67%)	112 (56%)	29 (41.42%)	99 (49.5%)	21 (30%)	99 (49.5%)
Currency	98 (49%)	107 (53.5%)	101 (50.5%)	89 (44.5%)	12 (17.14%)	87 (43.5%)	17 (24.28%)	87 (43.5%)
Authority	132 (66%)	122 (61%)	134 (67%)	107 (53.5%)	24 (34.28%)	126 (63%)	23 (32.85%)	125 (62.5%)
Mean	116.50	107.75	127.50	110.25	27.00	104.75	25.50	108.25
SD	14.20	10.05	17.97	18.10	12.83	16.38	10.63	18.32

(Multiple answers permitted)

Table 3.3.18 shows the criteria used for evaluating the information in print and electronic formats. Most of the research scholars of IITR 141 (70.5%) more than IIML 43 (61.42%), IIMI 41(58.57%) and IITD 115 (57.5%) indicated that they evaluate information on the basis of accuracy while the majority of the postgraduate students of IITR 133 (66.5%) more than IIMI 122 (61%), IIML 107 (53.5%) and IITD 99 (49.5%) evaluate information on the basis of accuracy. A high percentage of IITR 134 (67%) more than IITD 121 (60.5%), IIML 29 (41.42%) and IIMI 21(30%) indicated that they evaluate information on the basis of relevancy whereas postgraduate students of IITR 112 (56%) more than IITD 103 (51.5%), and IIML and IIMI 99 (49.5%) evaluated information on the basis of relevancy. The majority of the research scholars of IITR 101 (50.5%) more than IITD 98 (49%), IIMI 17 (24%) and 12 (17.14%) indicated that they evaluate information on the basis of currency while postgraduate students of IITD 107 (53.5%) more than IITR 89 (44.5%), IIML and IIMI 87 (43.5%) evaluated information on the basis of currency. The number of research scholars of IITR 134 (67%) more than IITD 132 (66%), IIMI 23 (32.85%) and IIML 24 (34.28%) indicated that they evaluate information on the basis of authority while postgraduate students of IIML 126 (63%) more than IIMI 125 (62.5%), IITD 122 (61%) and IITR 107 (53.5%) evaluated information on the basis of authority.

Statistical Inference

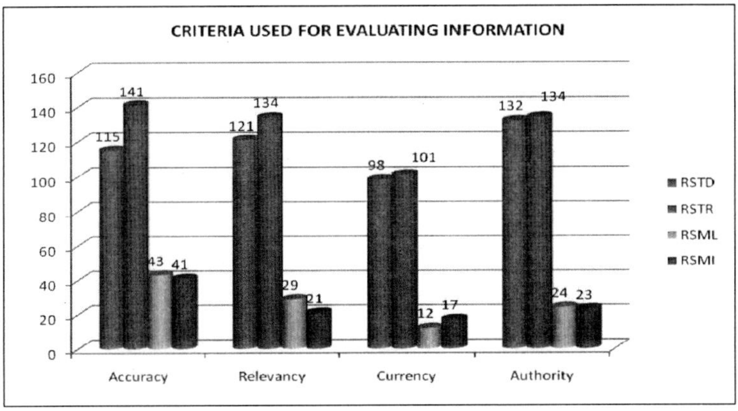

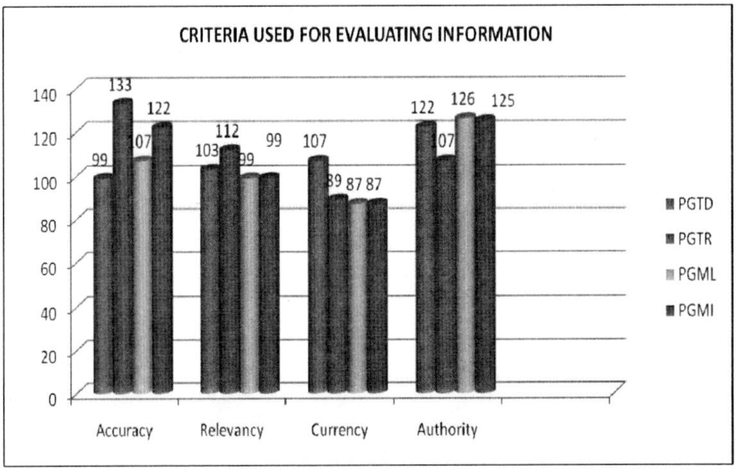

It can be interpreted from the table 3.3.18 that "Authority and Currency" of the web resources was revealed to be the most important criteria in the evaluation of web resources among resources of IITs researchers. However, in IIMs research scholars *checked* the 'Accuracy' *credentials* for evaluating the authority of web resources the accuracy.

Table 3.3.19:
Assessment Tools to Determine Information Literacy Competency

Response	IITD		IITR		IIML		IIMI	
	RS N=200	PGS N=200	RS N=200	PGS N=200	RS N=70	PGS N=200	RS N=70	PGS N=200
Yes	7 3.5%)	4 (2%)	132 (66%)	119 (59.5%)	39 (55.71%)	137 (68.5%)	5 (7.14%)	9 (4.5%)
No	193 (96.5%)	196 (98%)	68 (34%)	81 (40.5%)	31 (44.28%)	63 (31.5%)	65 (92.85%)	191 (95.5%)
Mean	100.00	100.00	100.00	100.00	35.00	100.00	35.00	100.00
SD	131.52	135.76	45.25	26.87	5.66	52.33	42.43	128.69

Table 3.3.19 shows the assessment tools to determine information literacy competency in the users of selected libraries. It is observed from Table 3.3.19 that the majority of the research scholars of IITR 132 (66%) more than IIML 39 (55.71%) indicated that they have assessment tools to determine information literacy competency while postgraduate students of IIML 137 (68.5%) more than IITR 119 (59.5%) indicated that they have assessment tools to determine information literacy competency. The majority of research scholars and postgraduate students of IITD and IIMI indicated that they do not have any assessment tools to determine information literacy competency in the users.

Statistical Inference

Table 3.3.19 means score shows that, the highest number of responses above the mean were "assessment tools to determine information literacy competency" While, the mean score received for RS and PGS, IITD (RS) (Mean=100.0, SD=131.52), IITD (PGS) (Mean=100.0, SD=135.76), IITR (RS) (Mean=100.0, SD=45.25), IITR (PGS) (Mean=100.0, SD=26.87), IIML (RS) (Mean=35.00, SD=5.66), IIML (PGS) (Mean=100.0, SD= 52.33),

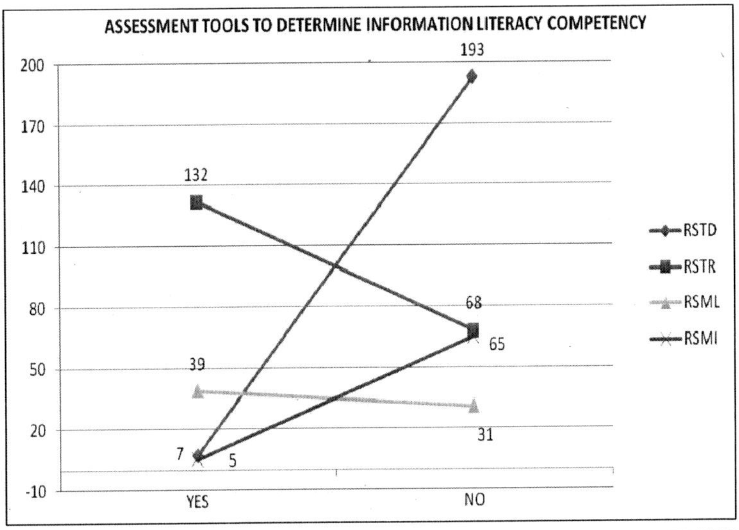

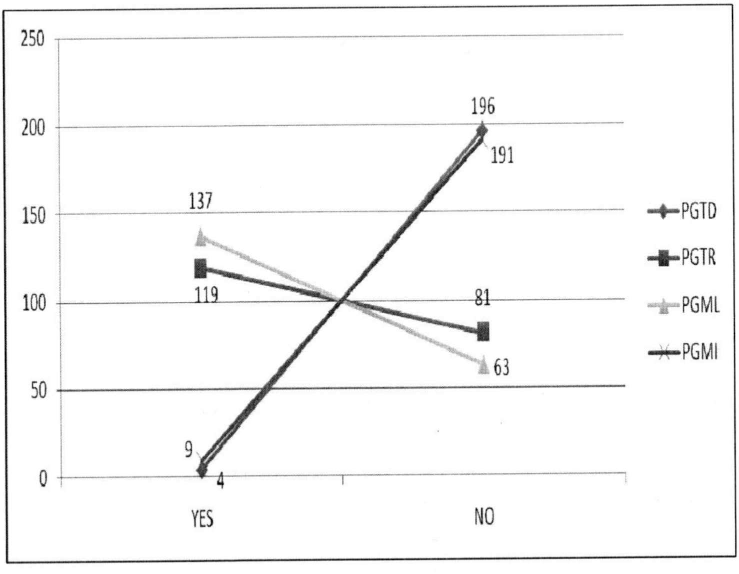

Table 3.3.20: Hindrances Encountered by Respondents in ILP

Hindrances	IITD		IITR		IIML		IIMI	
	RS N=200	PGS N=200	RS N=200	PGS N=200	RS N=70	PGS N=200	RS N=70	PGS N=200
Lack of staff	40 (20%)	37 (18.5%)	53 (26.5%)	42 (21%)	14 (20%)	42 (21%)	18 (25.71%)	65 (32.5%)
Lack of trained staff	31 (15.5%)	42 (21%)	23 (11.5%)	28 (14%)	11 (15.71%)	34 (17%)	9 (12.85%)	26 (13%)
Lack of finance	36 (18%)	32 (16%)	43 (21.5%)	39 (19.5%)	19 (27.14%)	23 (11.5%)	14 (20%)	21 (10.5%)
Lack of administrative support	43 (21.5%)	21 (10.5%)	25 (12.5%)	32 (16%)	19 (27.14%)	34 (17%)	23 (32.85%)	33 (16.5%)
Lack of policy matter	49 (24.5%)	64 (32%)	53 (26.5%)	34 (17%)	9 (12.85%)	31 (15.5%)	21 (30%)	58 (29%)
Mean	39.80	39.20	39.40	35.00	14.40	32.80	17.00	40.60
SD	6.83	15.90	14.66	5.57	4.56	6.83	5.61	19.71

(Multiple answers were permitted)

IIMI (RS) (Mean=35.00, SD=42.43), IIMI (PGS) (Mean=100.0, SD=128.69).

Information literacy has become a common tool among the academic communities. Respondents still face a various problems when accessing information resources. Table 3.3.20 shows that research scholars of IITR 53 (26.5%) found the problem of lack of staff more than IIMI 18 (25.71%), IITD and IIML 40 (20%) in organizing information literacy programmes while postgraduate students of IIMI 65 (32.5%), IITR and IIML 42 (21%), and IITD 37 (18.5%) found the problem of lack of staff. The majority of research scholars of IIMI 23 (32.85%) more than IIML 19 (27.14%), IITD 43 (21.5%), and IITR 25 (12.5%) found the problem of the lack of administrative support while postgraduate students of IIML 34 (17%) more than IITR 32 (16%), IIMI 33 (16.5%) and IITD 21 (10.5%) found the problem of organizing ILP.

The maximum research scholars of IIMI 21 (30%) more than IITR 53 (26.5%), IITD 49 (24.5%) and IIML 9 (12.85%) found the problem of lack of policy matters while postgraduate students of IITD 64 (32%) more than IIMI 58 (29%), IITR 34 (17%), IIML 31 (15.5%) found the problem of lack of policy matters in organizing ILP.

Statistical Inference

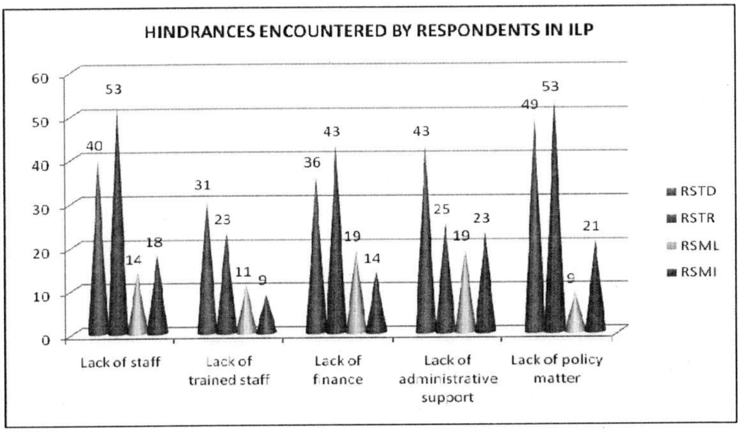

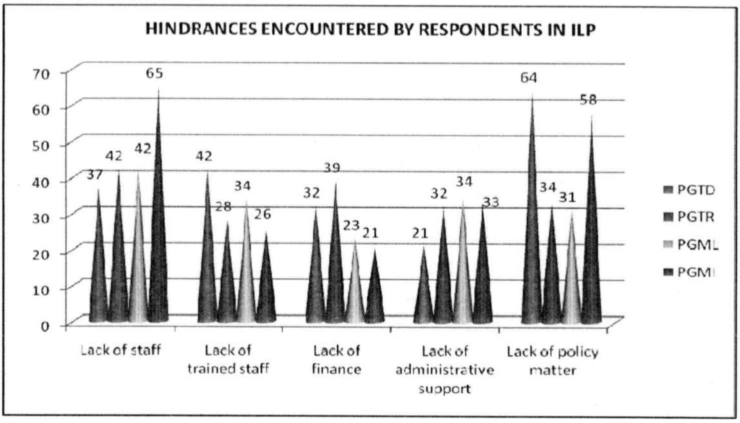

Table number 3.3.20 shows that the maximum number of RS (49) and IITD (PGS) (64) responses were obtained for the option 'Lack of policy matter" in case of IITD whereas, the least number of RS (9) of response were received for the option 'Lack of trained staff/ Lack of policy matter'. A similarity was observed in IITR, IIML and IIMI.

Table 3.3.21: Satisfaction Level of the Respondents

Satisfaction Level	IITD		IITR		IIML		IIMI	
	RS N=200	PGS N=200	RS N=200	PGS N=200	RS N=70	PGS N=200	RS N=70	PGS N=200
Very satisfied	87 (43.5%)	62 (31%)	69 (34.5%)	59 (29.5%)	18 (25.71%)	74 (37%)	38 (54.28%)	134 (67%)
Moderately satisfied	79 (39.5%)	83 (41.5%)	64 (32%)	75 (37.5%)	35 (50%)	59 (29.5%)	23 (32.85%)	46 (23%)
Dissatisfied	34 (17%)	55 (27.5%)	67 (33.5%)	66 (33%)	17 (24.29%)	67 (33.5%)	9 (12.87%)	20 (10%)
Total	200 (100%)	200 (100%)	200 (100%)	200 (100%)	70 (100%)	200 (100%)	70 (100%)	200 (100%)
Mean	66.67	66.67	66.67	66.67	23.33	66.67	23.33	66.67
SD	28.57	14.57	2.52	8.02	10.12	7.51	14.50	59.74

It is important to know the satisfaction level of research scholars and postgraduate students with the present information literacy programmes of the selected libraries. Table

3.3.21 shows that the majority of the research scholars of IIMI 38 (54.28%), IITD 87 (43.5%), IITR 69 (34.5%), IIML 18 (25.71%) were very satisfied with the present information literacy programmes of the library while postgraduate students of IIMI 134 (67%), IIML 74 (37%), IITD 62 (31%), and IITR 59 (29.5%) were very satisfied with the present information literacy programmes of the library. The maximum research scholars of IIML 35 (50%), IITD 79 (39.5%), IITR 64 (32%), IIMI 23 (32.85%) were moderately satisfied with the present information literacy programmes of the library while postgraduate students of IITD 83 (41.5%), IITR 75 (37.5%), IIML 59 (29.5%), and IIMI 46 (23%) were moderately satisfied with the present information literacy programmes. It is found that research scholars of IITR 67 (33.5%), IIML 17 (24.29%), IITD 34 (17%), IIMI 9 (12.87%) were dissatisfied with the present information literacy programmes of the library while postgraduate students of IIML 67 (33.5%), IITR 66 (33%), IITD 55 (27.5%), and IIMI 20 (10%) were dissatisfied with the present information literacy programmes of the library.

Statistical Inference

The statistical analysis of the data shows that highest satisfaction level (very satisfied) observed among the researchers from IITs and IIMs based on Mean (66.67). Whereas, majority of PGS were 'Moderately satisfied' based on

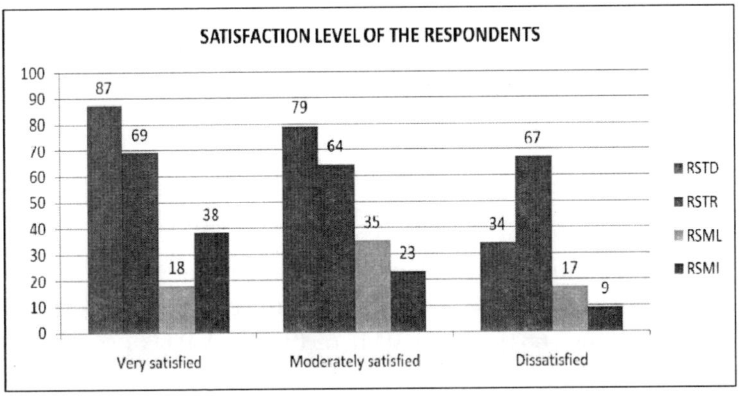

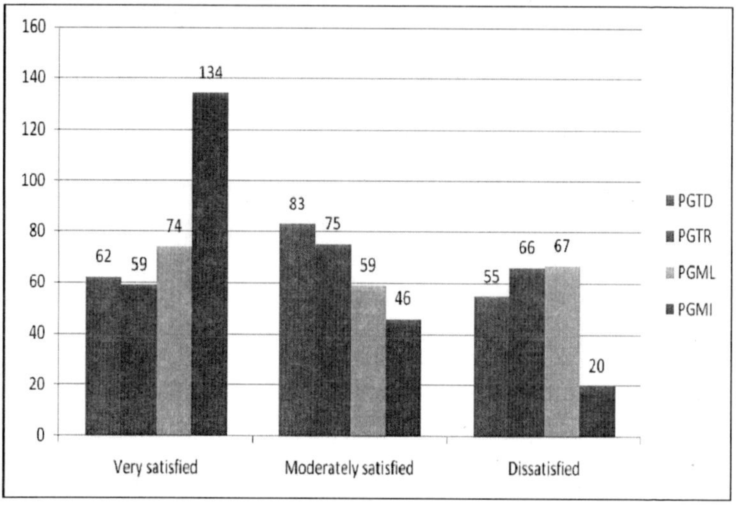

percentage. PGS of IIMI PGS (67%). The obtained Mean signifies that overall the researchers of the four institutes under study were satisfied with the quality of information retrieved through the web.

Table 3.3.22: Need of Training

Response	IITD		IITR		IIML		IIMI	
	RS N=200	PGS N=200	RS N=200	PGS N=200	RS N=70	PGS N=200	RS N=70	PGS N=200
Yes	173 (86.5%)	184 (92%)	169 (84.5%)	187 (93.5%)	65 (92.86%)	182 (91%)	68 (97.14%)	179 (89.5%)
No	27 (13.5%)	16 (8%)	31 (15.5%)	13 (6.5%)	5 (7.14%)	18 (9%)	2 (2.86%)	21 (10.5%)
Mean	100.00	100.00	100.00	100.00	35.00	100.00	35.00	100.00
SD	103.24	118.79	97.58	123.04	42.43	115.97	46.67	111.72

The respondents were asked whether they need training to make maximum use of information resources and library services. Table 3.3.22 shows that the majority of the research scholars of IIMI 68 (97.14%), IIML 65 (92.86%), IITD 173 (86.5%), and IITR 169 (84.5%) were in favour of imparting training while postgraduate students of IITR 187 (93.5%), IITD 184 (92%), IIML 182 (91%), IIMI 179 (89.5%) were in favour of imparting training. It was also found that the research scholars of IITR 31 (15.5%), IITD 27 (13.5%), IIML 18 (9%), IIMI 2 (2.86%) knew how to use resources and services of the library, so they did not need training while postgraduate students of IIMI 21 (10.5%), IIML 18 (9%), IITD 16 (8%), IITR 13 (6.5%) were not in favor of training.

Statistical Inference

The highest number of response was obtained for hands on training in all the four institutes under study i.e. (RS : 173,169,65,68 and PGS:184,187,182,179) in IITD, IITR, IIML and IIMI respectively which was quite above the mean score. The mean score of IITD, IITR, IIML and IIMI was observed to be 100.0 (SD=103.24), 100.0 (SD=97.58), 35.0 (SD=42.43) and 35.0 (SD=46.67). The lowest response below the average score was obtained for the option 'I do not need any training'.

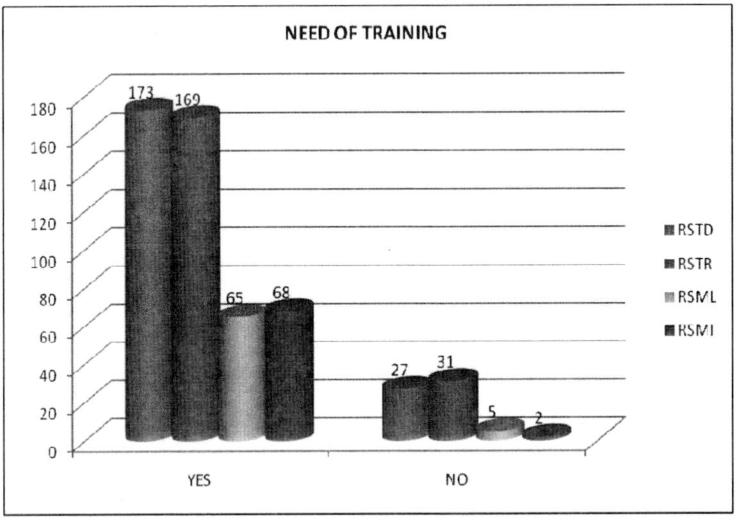

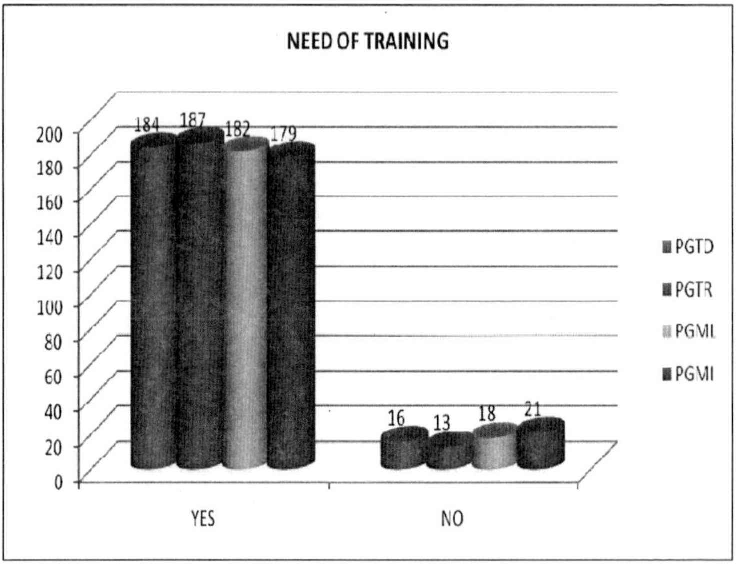
NEED OF TRAINING
200
180
160
140
120
100
80
60
40
20
0
184
187
182
179
16
13
18
21
YES
NO
PGTD
PGTR
PGML
PGMI

4

Findings, Tenability of Hypothesis, Conclusion and Suggestions

This chapter presents the major findings, which have been drawn on the basis of data collected from the four institutes under the study. Tenability of the hypotheses is checked with the help of independent t-test as a statistical tool and suggestions are provided to improve the information literacy skills in research scholars and PG students in the IIT and IIM libraries. At the end some recommendation and possible areas for further research also have been mentioned in this chapter.

4.1 SUMMARY OF FINDINGS

The study intends to know the status of information literacy competencies among research scholars and postgraduate students of selected IIT and IIM libraries. The major findings of the study are identified on the basis of data received from the users and the working librarians. The major findings of the study are:

4.1.1 Librarians' Views

On the basis of data analysis of librarians' responses, the following findings have been derived:

1. Table 3.1.2 indicates that IIT, Roorkee and IIM, Indore have a full-time librarian, whereas IIT, Delhi, and IIM, Lucknow have an in-charge librarian. Further categorized the strength of total staff in these four

libraries, IIT, Roorkee has maximum staff such as (24), followed by (18) in IIT, Delhi, (16) in IIM, Indore, and 13 staff in IIM, Lucknow.

2. Table 3.1.3 shows that the total collection IIT, Delhi has the highest, i.e.13.2 lakhs in print form and 1.6 lakhs in electronic form, followed by IIT, Roorkee has 4.5 lakhs in print form and 65,000 in electronic form. Similarly, IIM, Indore has 37,878 in print form and 2.7 lakhs in electronic form and IIM, Lucknow has 45,470 in print form and 166,856 in electronic form.
3. Table 3.1.4 indicates that IIT, Delhi has the highest number of registered users such as 4582, in which 1597 users are research scholars and 2985 are postgraduate students followed by IIT, Roorkee has 4520, in which 1352 research scholars and 3168 postgraduate students similarly IIM, Indore has 1223, in which 106 research scholars and 1117 postgraduate student and IIM, Lucknow has 1000, in which 80 research scholars and 920 postgraduate students registered.
4. Table 3.1.5 clearly indicates the current annual budget (2015-16) of selected libraries. IIT, Roorkee has the highest annual budget, i.e. (15.4 crore), followed by IIT, Delhi Library, i.e. (14.25 crore), IIM, Lucknow, i.e. (3.75 crore), and IIM, Indore has the lowest annual budget, i.e. (3.4 crore).
5. Table 3.1.6 shows these three libraries, i.e. IIT, Delhi, IIT, Roorkee, and IIM, Lucknow use LIBSYS software followed by IIM, Indore uses VIRTUA software.
6. Table 3.2.4 shows IIT, Delhi has prior agenda while organizing ILP to attract students towards the library and optimize the usage of library resources followed by IIT, Roorkee and IIM, Lucknow have most prior agenda while organizing ILP to attract students towards the library, optimize the usage of library resources, and ability to retrieve data for their

assignments efficiently. IIM, Indore has one prior agenda while organizing ILP to develop the ability to retrieve data for their assignments efficiently.

7. It is observed that IITD and IITR libraries covered all related topics in information literacy instructions. Similarly, IIML and IIMI libraries covered topics in information literacy instruction slightly less.
8. The study revealed that IIML has an assessment tool to determine student information literacy competency. Similarly, IITD, IITR, and IIMI have not any assessment tools to determine student information competency.
9. Table 3.2.12 depicts that IL instruction methods were used by the selected libraries. It is clear from table 3.2.12 that IIM, Indore used all IL instruction methods, i.e. face-to-face, workshop/seminars, online/web-based tutorials, combination of online and face-to-face, printed training manuals, individual instruction at the reference desk for the users. Similarly, IIT, Delhi used IL instruction methods, i.e. face-to-face, workshop/ seminars, Online/web-based tutorials, individual instruction at the reference desk and IITR provided IL instruction, i.e. face-to-face, workshop/seminars, online/web-based tutorials, combination of online and face-to-face, printed training manuals, individual instruction at the reference desk, whereas IIM, Lucknow used only two IL instruction methods, i.e. face-to-face and individual instruction at the reference desk for their users. It indicates that the majority of libraries, i.e. IIM, Indore, IIT, Roorkee, and IIT, Delhi felt that providing better information literacy instruction methods to the users will increase the proper utilization of library resources and services.

4.1.2 User's Performs

A separate questionnaire has been distributed to find out the user's viewpoint about information literacy skills. This part shows major findings on the basis of the analysis and interpretation of the collected data received from users in the IIM and IIT libraries under study:

- Majority of researchers in IIMI (55.71%) visit to the Library daily, similarly in IIML (52.85%), IITD (48.5%) and IITR (43.5%). It can also be seen m table that majority of PGS in IITD (26%) visit to the library daily, similarly in IIML (23.5%), IITR (22.7%) and IIMI (22.5%). It is also visible from the study that monthly visit to the library by RS of IITR (21.5%) is more than RS of IITD (16.5%), IIML (12.87%) and IIMI (18.57%).
- Response received from the users indicated that the major purpose of information needed by the RS in different institutions admitted using information needed for research work, (71.5%), (69%), (70%) and (68.57%) in IITD, IITR,IIML and IIMI respectively,. Table data also shows low percentage of information needed by PG students, (27%) in IITR, (25.5%) in IITD, (29.5%) in IIML and (18.5%) in IIMI, admitted using information needed for research work.
- Researchers and PG students work always involves keeping abreast of the recent developments in their respective fields and it can be clearly depicted from the table 4.3.3 that, a percentage of the researchers from the select institutes under the study acknowledged using purpose of information needed by the RS to be research work for Assignment i.e. (26.50%) in IITD, (19%) in IITR, (25.71%) in IIML and (20%) in IIMI.
- The majority of research scholars frequently used information sources for theses/Dissertation moreover (87.5%) in IITD, in IITR (73.5%), IIML (61.42%) and IIMI (55.71%). On the other hand the PG students frequently used information sources for Textbooks (90.5%) in IITD, (82.5%) in IITR, (86%) in IIML and (88.5%) in IIMI.

- Majority of IITR RS respond "familiarity with information literacy" is maximum (82%), IITD RS and IIML RS (69%), IIMI (58.57%). In contrast, IITD PG students familiarity with information literacy moreover (77%), (59.5%) in IITR, (68.5%) in IIML and (64.5%) in IIMI.
- It is observed that research scholars and PG students of IITD, IITR, IIML and IIMI prefer Print medium to access information.
- It reveals that number of research scholars of IIML and IIMI (58.57%) rated their skills highly in printing document files, IITR (62.5%) in opening and saving files, IIMI (61.42%) in making spreadsheets, IIMI (60%) in copying and transferring files, IIMI (58.57%) in drawing pictures rated their skills highly except for power point presentations rated their skills as average, whereas postgraduate students of IIMI (54%), IITR (64.5%), IIMI (67%), IIML (49%) rated their skills highly in printing document files, opening and saving files, copying and transferring files and picture drawing. The majority of postgraduate students of IIML (58.58%) and IIMI (55%), IITR (49.5%) and IITD (48.5%) rated their skill average in spreadsheet making and IIMI (50.5%) rated their skills as average in Power Point presentations.
- It is observed that postgraduate students were more familiar with Facebook, and WhatsApp than the research scholars. Thus, they were able to make use of these social media platforms for their services.
- It reveals that Google Chrome was more used as browser 38 (54.28%), while the least used browser was Opera 5 (2.5%).
- It is observed that research scholars of IITD (31.5%) prefer "Title" for locating documents on shelves, in contrast research scholars of IITR (28.5%) prefer "Subject" and RS of IIMs prefer "Call number" with

(44.28%), (35.71%) IIML, IIMI respectively. In PGS responses, trend is in contrast. None of institutions PGS prefer "Title". The responses of PGS institutions prefer "Subject" with (33.5%), 29.5%), (32.5%) and (33.5%) of IITD, IITR, IIML and IIMI respectively.

- It reveals that the field search (title, author, subject, etc.) were used more by the research scholars and postgraduate students than simple search, and Boolean operators were used less by research scholars and postgraduate students for searching documents.
- It reveals from the study that the research scholars of IITR 88 (44%) rated their skills as average than IIML 27 (38.57%), IITD 71 (35.5%) and IIMI 19 (27.4%) while postgraduate students of IITR 93 (46.5%) more than IITD 92 (46%), IIMI 88 (44%) and IIML 67 (33.5%) rated their skills as average in downloading scholarly articles. The number of research scholars of IIML 31 (44.28%) and IIMI 30 (42.85%) rated their skills highly for searching in Web OPAC while that majority of postgraduate student of IITR 95 (47.5%), IITD 91 (45.5%), IIML 90 (45%) and IIMI 87 (43.5%) rated themselves as low. Most of the research scholars of IITD 89 (44.5%) and IITR 81 (40.5%) rated their skills as average for searching in Web OPAC.
- It is observed that research scholars and PG students do not have a proper awareness regarding information literacy standards, guidelines, and policies.
- It reveals that the highest number of research scholars and PG students participated at the starting of the academic year in the information literacy programmes and the lowest number of responses were observed in case of monthly basis.
- It is observed that the 118 (59%) of research scholars and 98 (49%) of postgraduate students of IITD, whereas the librarian takes responsibility for delivering

information literacy programmes. On the other hand, 46 (23%) of research scholars of IITR and 55 (27.5%) of postgraduate students of IITD, where, both librarian and faculty are responsible for conducting information literacy programmes in their library.

- It is identified that majority of research scholars and PG students of selected IIT and IIM libraries attended information literacy programmes organized by the libraries.
- It reveals from the table 3.3.18 that "Authority and Currency" of the web resources was revealed to be the most important criteria in the evaluation of web resources among resources of IITs researchers. However, in IIMs research scholars *checked* the "Accuracy" *credentials* for evaluating the authority of web resources the accuracy.
- It is identified that majority of the research scholars of IITR 132 (66%) more than IIML 39 (55.71%) indicated that they have assessment tools to determine information literacy competency while postgraduate students of IIML 137 (68.5%) more than IITR 119 (59.5%) indicated that they have assessment tools to determine information literacy competency. It is also reveals from the study that research scholars and postgraduate students of IITD and IIMI indicated that they do not have any assessment tools to determine information literacy competency in the users.
- It reveals that the maximum number of RS (49) and IITD (PGS) (64) responses were obtained for the option 'Lack of policy matter" in case of IITD whereas, the least number of RS (9) of response were received for the option 'Lack of trained staff/ Lack of policy matter'. A similarity was observed in IITR, IIML and IIMI.
- The statistical analysis of the data shows that highest satisfaction level (very satisfied) observed among the

researchers from IITs and IIMs. Whereas, majority of PGS were 'Moderately satisfied' based on percentage. PGS of IIMI PGS (67%). The obtained Mean signifies that overall the researchers of the four institutes under study were satisfied with the quality of information retrieved through the web.

- The respondents were asked whether they need training to make maximum use of information resources and library services. It reveals from the study that majority of the research scholars of IIMI 68 (97.14%), IIML 65 (92.86%), IITD 173 (86.5%), and IITR 169 (84.5%) were in favour of imparting training while postgraduate students slightly less in favour of imparting training.

4.2 TENABILITY OF HYPOTHESIS

A thorough analysis of previous research investigations and related literature has been significant in formulating the hypothesis for the present study. In the light of findings the tenability of hypothesis formulated for the study is checked and is presented below:

Hypothesis No. 1

H0: The users have considerable awareness of different sources of information.

It is evident from the Table 3.3.4 that the research scholars and postgraduate students were able to identify the appropriate sources of information for their study purposes. Awareness of different sources of information, i.e. textbooks, reference books, journals, newsletters, theses, dissertations, conference and seminar proceedings, Wikipedia, online databases, e-journals, e-books.

For verification of above data, respondent has applied t-test at 95% confidence interval percentage.

t-test

Institutes		Mean	Std. Deviation	Std. Error Mean	F	Sig.	t	Sig. (2-tailed)
RS	IITD	127.25	36.058	127.25	.654	.432	.074	.942
	IITR	126.00	31.555	126.00				
PG	IITD	80.50	52.745	80.50	.325	.578	.749	.466
	IITR	61.88	46.508	61.88				
RS	IIML	35.88	7.918	35.88	1.829	.198	-.408	.690
	IIMI	38.38	15.436	38.38				
PG	IIML	64.75	52.993	64.75	.373	.551	.130	.898
	IIMI	61.25	54.717	61.25				

(RSTD: IITD(RS), RSTR: IITR(RS), PGTD: IITD(PG), PGTR: IITR(PG), RSML: IITML(RS), RSMI: IIMI(RS), PGML: IIML(PG), PGMI: IIMI(PG)

From the above test result, it is clear that significance value (p) of IIT(s) and IIM(s) combination(s) are more than .05, which shows, there is no statistically significant difference between different resources of four institutes.

The table 3.3.6 shows that most of the research scholars of IIT, Delhi (61.5%) than 60% of IIM, Lucknow, 58.57% of IIM, Indore and 46% of IIT, Roorkee rated their skills highly in accessing information in print format. On the other hand postgraduate students of IIT, Delhi (61%) more than 56.5% of IIM, Lucknow 53.5% of IIM, Indore and 48.5% of IIT, Roorkee rated their skills highly for accessing information in print format.

It is clear from the study that for accessing information in print format, the majority of the research scholars and postgraduate students rated their skills highly. Therefore on the basis of the above mentioned results this hypothesis is **proved.**

Hypothesis No. 2

H0: The users have considerable awareness of search strategies and techniques for accessing the required information.

It is clear from Table 3.3.12 that research scholars and postgraduate students' awareness regarding search strategies and techniques were found not significantly different.

t-test

Institutes		Mean	Std. Deviation	Std. Error Mean	F	Sig.	t	Sig. (2-tailed)
RS	IITD	50.00	25.364	12.682	.022	.888	.000	1.000
	IITR	50.00	26.658	13.329				
PG	IITD	50.00	24.536	12.268	1.948	.212	.000	1.000
	IITR	50.00	18.166	9.083				
RS	IIML	17.50	10.970	5.485	.483	.513	.000	1.000
	IIMI	17.50	11.619	5.809				
PG	IIML	50.00	34.986	17.493	.397	.552	.000	1.000
	IIMI	50.00	32.228	16.114				

(RSTD: IITD(RS), RSTR: IITR(RS), PGTD: IITD(PG), PGTR: IITR(PG), RSML: IITML(RS), RSMI: IIMI(RS), PGML: IIML(PG), PGMI: IIMI(PG)

For verification of above data, researcher and PGS have applied t-test at 95% confidence interval percentage.

From the above test result, it is clear that significance value (p) of IIT(s) and IIM(s) combination(s) are more than .05, so there is no statistically significant difference between different resources of four institutes.

It is evident from table 3.3.10 that the maximum research scholars and PG students of IIT and IIM libraries were more familiar with search engines.

It is clear from the table 3.3.11 that all these responses indicate that research scholars and postgraduate students of IIMI and IIML were more familiar with the call number for locating documents on the shelves than the research scholars and postgraduate students of IITR and IITD. Most of the postgraduate students, 67 (33.5%) of IITD and IIMI, 65 (32.5%) of IIML, 59 (29.5%) of IITR indicated that they searched for books according to the subject of the book while research scholars, 60 (30%) of IITD, 57 (28.5%) IITR, 19 (27.14%) of IIMI and 18 (25.73%) searched for books according to the subject of the books. Therefore this hypothesis gets **accepted.**

Hypothesis No. 3

H0: Researchers and postgraduate students are able to use appropriate methods as evaluation criteria while selecting the required information for their study purposes.

It is evident from the Tables 3.3.18 that, the majority of the respondents were more aware of criteria for evaluating information while selecting the required information.

t-test

Institutes		Mean	Std. Deviation	Std. Error Mean	F	Sig.	t	Sig. (2-tailed)
RS	IITD	116.50	14.201	7.100	.269	.623	-.960	.374
	IITR	127.50	17.972	8.986				
PG	IITD	107.75	10.046	5.023	.654	.450	-.242	.817
	IITR	110.25	18.099	9.050				
RS	IIML	27.00	12.832	6.416	.070	.801	.180	.863
	IIMI	25.50	10.630	5.315				
PG	IIML	104.75	16.378	8.189	.447	.529	-.285	.785
	IIMI	108.25	18.319	9.159				

(RSTD: IITD(RS), RSTR: IITR(RS), PGTD: IITD(PG), PGTR: IITR(PG), RSML: IITML(RS), RSMI: IIMI(RS), PGML: IIML(PG), PGMI: IIMI(PG)

For verification of above data, respondent has applied t-test at 95% confidence interval percentage.

From the above test result, it is clear that significance value (p) of IIT(s) and IIM(s) combination(s) are more than .05, so there is no statistically significant difference between different resources of four institutes. Therefore, on the basis of the above findings this hypothesis is **proved.**

Hypothesis No. 4

H0: The majority of the users are able to retrieve the required information from the sources.

It is clear from the table that all these responses indicate that research scholars and postgraduate students of IIMI and IIML were more familiar with the call number for locating documents on the shelves than the research scholars and postgraduate students of IITR and IITD. Most of the

t-test

Institutes		Mean	Std. Deviation	Std. Error Mean	F	Sig.	t	Sig. (2-tailed)
RS	IITD	50.00	13.342	6.671	14.520	.009	.000	1.000
	IITR	50.00	7.394	3.697				
PG	IITD	50.00	16.432	8.216	.006	.943	.000	1.000
	IITR	50.00	16.693	8.347				
RS	IIML	17.50	9.747	4.873	.411	.545	.000	1.000
	IIMI	17.50	7.047	3.524				
PG	IIML	50.00	16.793	8.396	.016	.903	.000	1.000
	IIMI	50.00	16.852	8.426				

(RSTD: IITD(RS), RSTR: IITR(RS), PGTD: IITD(PG), PGTR: IITR(PG), RSML: IITML(RS), RSMI: IIMI(RS), PGML: IIML(PG), PGMI: IIMI(PG)

postgraduate students, 67 (33.5%) of IITD and IIMI, 65 (32.5%) of IIML, 59 (29.5%) of IITR indicated that they searched for books according to the subject of the book while research scholars, 60 (30%) of IITD, 57 (28.5%) IITR, 19 (27.14%) of IIMI and 18 (25.73%) searched for books according to the subject of the books.

It is clear from Table 3.3.9 that respondents awareness of call numbers were no significantly different from finding to find a document on shelves in the library.

For verification of above data, researcher and PGS have applied t-test at 95% confidence interval percentage.

From the above test result, it is clear that significance value (p) of IIT(s) and IIM(s) combination(s) are more than .05, so there is no statistically significant difference between different resources of four institutes. Therefore, on the basis of above result hypothesis is **proved.**

Hypothesis No. 5

H0: Research scholars and postgraduate students need more training assistance and guidance on how to use and access electronic and print information resources.

The respondents were asked whether they need training to make maximum use of information resources and library services. It is evident from the table 3.3.22 shows that the majority of the research scholars of IIMI 68 (97.14%), IIML 65 (92.86%), IITD 173 (86.5%), and IITR 169 (84.5%) were in favour of imparting training while postgraduate students of IITR 187 (93.5%), IITD 184 (92%), IIML 182 (91%), IIMI 179 (89.5%) were in favour of imparting training. It was also found that the research scholars of IITR 31 (15.5%), IITD 27 (13.5%), IIML 18 (9%), IIMI 2 (2.86%) knew how to use resources and services of the library, so they did not need training while postgraduate students of IIMI 21 (10.5%), IIML 18 (9%), IITD 16 (8%), IITR 13 (6.5%) were not in favor of training.

(t-test)

Institutes		Mean	Std. Deviation	Std. Error Mean	F	Sig.	T	Sig. (2-tailed)
RS	IITD	100.00	103.238	73.000	.	.	.000	1.000
	IITR	100.00	97.581	69.000				
PG	IITD	100.00	118.794	84.000	.	.	.000	1.000
	IITR	100.00	123.037	87.000				
RS	IIML	35.00	42.426	30.000	.	.	.000	1.000
	IIMI	35.00	46.669	33.000				
PG	IIML	100.00	115.966	82.000	.	.	.000	1.000
	IIMI	100.00	111.723	79.000				

(RSTD: IITD(RS), RSTR: IITR(RS), PGTD: IITD(PG), PGTR: IITR(PG), RSML: IITML(RS), RSMI: IIMI(RS), PGML: IIML(PG), PGMI: IIMI(PG)

For verification of above data, respondent has applied t-test at 95% confidence interval percentage.

From the above test result, it is clear that significance value (p) of IIT(s) and IIM(s) combination(s) are more than .05, so there is no statistically significant difference between different resources of four institutes.

It is evident from the table 3.3.13 these findings suggest that the research scholars of IITR 88 (44%) rated their skills as average than IIML 27 (38.57%), IITD 71 (35.5%) and IIMI 19 (27.4%) while postgraduate students of IITR 93 (46.5%) more than IITD 92 (46%), IIMI 88 (44%) and IIML 67 (33.5%) rated their skills as average in downloading scholarly articles. The number of research scholars of IIML 31 (44.28%) and IIMI 30 (42.85%) rated their skills highly for searching in Web OPAC while that majority of postgraduate student of IITR 95 (47.5%), IITD 91 (45.5%), IIML 90 (45%) and IIMI 87 (43.5%) rated themselves as low. Most of the research scholars of IITD 89 (44.5%) and IITR 81 (40.5%) rated their skills as average for searching in Web OPAC.

t-test

Institutes		Mean	Std. Deviation	Std. Error Mean	F	Sig.	t	Sig. (2-tailed)
RS	IITD	95.83	21.094	8.612	.248	.629	.031	.976
	IITR	95.50	16.134	6.587				
RS	IITD	82.50	7.477	3.052	4.370	.063	-.600	.562
	IITR	84.50	3.271	1.335				
RS	IITD	21.67	20.245	8.265	.653	.438	.153	.881
	IITR	20.00	17.367	7.090				
PG	IITD	85.83	19.488	7.956	.010	.922	.279	.786
	IITR	82.67	19.846	8.102				
PG	IITD	86.00	13.594	5.550	1.762	.214	.729	.483
	IITR	79.50	17.097	6.980				
PG	IITD	33.00	31.787	12.977	.045	.836	.000	.789
	IITR	37.83	29.055	11.861				
RS	IIML	39.83	5.913	2.414	.045	.836	.000	1.000
	IIMI	39.83	6.178	2.522				
RS	IIML	25.50	2.074	.847	1.116	.316	3.288	.008
	IIMI	20.67	2.944	1.202				
RS	IIML	4.67	5.354	2.186	1.691	.223	-1.197	.259
	IIMI	9.50	8.313	3.394				
PG	IIML	50.00	34.986	17.493	.378	.552	.124	.904
	IIMI	83.17	18.883	7.709				
PG	IIML	80.83	14.621	5.969	.353	.566	-.206	.841
	IIMI	82.67	16.219	6.622				
PG	IIML	36.00	30.272	12.359	.134	.722	.020	.985
	IIMI	35.67	27.696	11.307				

(RSTD: IITD(RS), RSTR: IITR(RS), PGTD: IITD(PG), PGTR: IITR(PG), RSML: IITML(RS), RSMI: IIMI(RS), PGML: IIML(PG), PGMI: IIMI(PG)

For verification of above data, researcher and PGS have applied t-test at 95% confidence interval percentage.

From the above test result, it is clear that significance value (p) of IIT(s) all combination are more than .05, so there is no statistically significant difference between different resources of four institutes. Therefore, on the basis of the above results this hypothesis is **proved and accepted**.

Hypothesis No. 6

H0: The users are reasonably satisfied with the information literacy programmes offered by the libraries.

The statistical analysis of the data shows that highest satisfaction level (very satisfied) observed among the researchers from IITs and IIMs based on Mean (66.67). Whereas, majority of PGS were 'Moderately satisfied' based on percentage. The obtained Mean signifies that overall the researchers of the four institutes under study were satisfied with the quality of information literacy programmes.

t-test

<table>
<tr><th colspan="2">Institutes</th><th>Mean</th><th>Std. Deviation</th><th>Std. Error Mean</th><th>F</th><th>Sig.</th><th>t</th><th>Sig. (2-tailed)</th></tr>
<tr><td rowspan="2">RS</td><td>IITD</td><td>66.67</td><td>28.572</td><td>16.496</td><td rowspan="2">11.26
6</td><td rowspan="2">.028</td><td rowspan="2">.000</td><td rowspan="2">1.000</td></tr>
<tr><td>IITR</td><td>66.67</td><td>2.517</td><td>1.453</td></tr>
<tr><td rowspan="2">PG</td><td>IITD</td><td>66.67</td><td>14.572</td><td>8.413</td><td rowspan="2">1.625</td><td rowspan="2">.271</td><td rowspan="2">.000</td><td rowspan="2">1.000</td></tr>
<tr><td>IITR</td><td>66.67</td><td>8.021</td><td>4.631</td></tr>
<tr><td rowspan="2">RS</td><td>IIML</td><td>23.33</td><td>10.116</td><td>5.840</td><td rowspan="2">.153</td><td rowspan="2">.716</td><td rowspan="2">.000</td><td rowspan="2">1.000</td></tr>
<tr><td>IIMI</td><td>23.33</td><td>14.503</td><td>8.373</td></tr>
<tr><td rowspan="2">PG</td><td>IIML</td><td>66.67</td><td>7.506</td><td>4.333</td><td rowspan="2">8.417</td><td rowspan="2">.044</td><td rowspan="2">.000</td><td rowspan="2">1.000</td></tr>
<tr><td>IIMI</td><td>66.67</td><td>59.744</td><td>34.493</td></tr>
</table>

(RSTD: IITD(RS), RSTR: IITR(RS), PGTD: IITD(PG), PGTR: IITR(PG), RSML: IITML(RS), RSMI: IIMI(RS), PGML: IIML(PG), PGMI: IIMI(PG)

For verification of above data, respondent has applied t-test at 95% confidence interval percentage.

From the above test result, it is clear that significance value (p) of IIT(s) and IIM(s) combination(s) are more than .05, so there is no statistically significant difference between different resources of four institutes.

It is evident from the table 3.3.17 shows that the majority of the research scholars of IITR 156 (78%), IIML 47 (67.14%), IITD 134 (67%), and IIMI 45 (64.28%) attended information literacy programmes while postgraduate students of IIML 147 (73.5%), ITD (145 (72.5%), IITR 137 (68.5%) and IIMI 134 (67%) attended information literacy programmes. It is found from the study that research scholars of IIMI 25 (35.72%), IITD 66 (33%), IIML 23 (32.86%) and IITR 44 (22%) did not attend information literacy programmes while postgraduate students of IIMI 66 (33%), IITR 63 (31.5%), IITD 55 (27.5%) and IIML 53 (26.5%) did not attend the information literacy programmes.

t-test

<table>
<tr><th colspan="2">Institutes</th><th>Mean</th><th>Std. Deviation</th><th>Std. Error Mean</th><th>F</th><th>Sig.</th><th>t</th><th>Sig. (2-tailed)</th></tr>
<tr><td rowspan="2">RS</td><td>IITD</td><td>100.00</td><td>48.083</td><td>34.000</td><td rowspan="2">.</td><td rowspan="2">.</td><td rowspan="2">.000</td><td rowspan="2">1.000</td></tr>
<tr><td>IITR</td><td>100.00</td><td>79.196</td><td>56.000</td></tr>
<tr><td rowspan="2">PG</td><td>IITD</td><td>100.00</td><td>63.640</td><td>45.000</td><td rowspan="2">.</td><td rowspan="2">.</td><td rowspan="2">.000</td><td rowspan="2">1.000</td></tr>
<tr><td>IITR</td><td>100.00</td><td>52.326</td><td>37.000</td></tr>
<tr><td rowspan="2">RS</td><td>IIML</td><td>35.00</td><td>16.971</td><td>12.000</td><td rowspan="2">.</td><td rowspan="2">.</td><td rowspan="2">.000</td><td rowspan="2">1.000</td></tr>
<tr><td>IIMI</td><td>35.00</td><td>14.142</td><td>10.000</td></tr>
<tr><td rowspan="2">PG</td><td>IIML</td><td>100.00</td><td>66.468</td><td>47.000</td><td rowspan="2">.</td><td rowspan="2">.</td><td rowspan="2">.000</td><td rowspan="2">1.000</td></tr>
<tr><td>IIMI</td><td>100.00</td><td>48.083</td><td>34.000</td></tr>
</table>

(RSTD: IITD(RS), RSTR: IITR(RS), PGTD: IITD(PG), PGTR: IITR(PG), RSML: IITML(RS), RSMI: IIMI(RS), PGML: IIML(PG), PGMI: IIMI(PG)

For verification of above data, respondent has applied t-test at 95% confidence interval percentage.

From the above test result, it is clear that significance value (p) of IIT(s) and IIM(s) combination(s) are more than .05, so there is no statistically significant difference between different resources of four institutes. On the basis of above findings this hypothesis is **proved to be true**.

4.3 SUGGESTIONS AND RECOMMENDATIONS

On the basis of findings consequent from the study, the view received from the librarians and users; and personal observation of the investigator, the following suggestions are made for improving and ensuring the information literacy competency in users of the libraries:

1. Librarians and authorities of the institute should insist on students attending library orientation to increase their awareness regarding organization of information and understanding of library tools, services, and resources.
2. The finance and other facilities should be provided by the libraries to organize the information literacy programmes.
3. It is suggested that users need orientated information literacy programmes which should be organized regularly.
4. There should be one compulsory library based assignment.
5. Information literacy Instruction should be integrated into the curriculum as a credit based score.
6. As it was found that users were not aware of search techniques and strategies, i.e. Boolean operators, field search, etc should be included and librarians should reinforce their learning.

7. There should be number of computers having good bandwidths with internet/intranet access available in the library for the users to provide faster access and better downloading speed and save the time of users.
8. Library Staff should be given adequate technical training from time to time to handle up with the latest updates in the technological development.
9. MHRD, UGC, and NAAC have identified information literacy instruction as one of the best practices. This should be converted into Information Literacy Policy.
10. It was found that users lacked awareness of the tools for retrieving the required documents. The librarian should collaborate with IT professionals and database vendors to make searching simple and easy.
11. It was found that the libraries do not have the assessment tools to determine information literacy competency in the users. Librarians should have the relevant tools which will help in designing effective information literacy programmes.
12. Collaboration between teachers and librarians is essential for enhancing the information literacy skills of the users.
13. Librarians and teachers should be trained for preparing information literacy programmes.

4.4 CONCLUSION

Researchers and PG students work always involves keeping abreast of the recent developments in their respective fields and it can be clearly depicted from the table 3.3.3 that, a percentage of the researchers from the select institutes under the study acknowledged using purpose of information needed by the RS to be research work for Assignment i.e. (26.50%) in IITD, (19%) in IITR, (25.71%) in IIML and (20%) in IIMI. For accessing information in electronic format, the majority of the research scholars of IIM, Lucknow and IIM, Indore (57.14%), 45% of IIT, Roorkee and 44.5% of IIT, Delhi rated their skills highly, whereas the majority of research scholars and postgraduate students were unfamiliar with search techniques and strategies, i.e. Boolean operators, field search (title, author, subject, etc.) used for searching in an online databases. Therefore, it was found that respondents faced difficulties with information retrieval tools like, call numbers, use of keywords and Boolean operators. It reveals from the study that postgraduate students were more familiar with Facebook, and WhatsApp than the research scholars. Thus, they were able to make use of these social media platforms for their services.

Everybody needs to develop information literacy and computer literacy competence. It was revealed from the study that institutes should develop assessment tools to determine information literacy competency for the users. The study also reveals that the majority of the respondents are able to identify and evaluate the required information. The study shows that an information literacy programme is inevitable for the research scholars and postgraduate students to make them more information literate. Information literacy instructions and training programmes needs to be organized on a regular basis due to the rapid growth of electronic and web-based information resources. Management and technology library professionals should do efforts to develop complete training programme or information literacy course not only for PG students and research scholars but for faculty members and UG students also, so that the existing gap between the capabilities and skills of the students and faculty can be improved. These training and instruction programmes should be revised and improved on regular basis. The library and information science professionals and teachers can do a lot to achieve this goal.

Appendices

Appendix-A

Questionnaire for Librarian

1. Please tick (✓) wherever appropriate.
2. Please fill the information in the blank space.
3. You may also provide more relevant information not included in the questionnaire, in a separate sheet if required.

PART-A: INSTITUTE/LIBRARY PROFILE

1. The Institute/Library
   i. Name and Address of the Library ....
   ....
   ....
   ....
   Phone No. .... Fax ....
   E-mail: ....
   Library Website ....
   ii. Head of the Library: Mr./Ms./Dr./Prof. ....
   ....
   ....
   Designation ....
   ....

2. Working Hours

Description	
Number of working days (approximately/ year)	
Opening hours (working days)	
Opening hours (Saturdays, Sundays and holidays)	

3. Library Collection

Items	Description	
	Print	Electronic
Books		
Current Journals		
Bound Journals		
PhD Thesis		
Online Databases		
Dissertations		
CD-ROMs		
Manuscripts		
Rare Books		
Audio Cassettes		
Videos		
Microfilms/Microfiches		
Magnetic Tapes/Films		
Others (Please specify)		

4. Library Staff

Designation	Strength
Librarian	
Deputy Librarians	
Assistant Librarians	

Information Scientist/Officers	
Professional Assistants	
Semi-Professional Assistants	
Library Assistants	
Technical Assistants	
Library Clerks	
Curators	
Library Attendants	
Others	

5. No. of Registered Library Users

Category of Users	**Strength**
Research Scholars	
Postgraduate Students	

6. Allocation of Annual Budget (2015-16)

S. No.	**Particular**	**Total (In Rs.)**
1.	Annual budget of the Information Literacy Programmes	
2.	Annual budget of the reading material (non-print)	
3.	Annual budget of the Information Technology, networking and automation work	
4.	Online journals, hardware and software	
5.	Others	
	Total	

7. Please state whether the library budget is:
   a. Adequate
   b. Fairly adequate
   c. Inadequate

8. Please state whether the budget for Library Information Literacy programmes are:
    a. Adequate
    b. Fairly adequate
    c. Inadequate

9. Which of the following housekeeping/automation software do you use in the library?
    a. SOUL
    b. KOHA
    c. LIBSYS
    d. E-Granthalaya
    e. NewGENLIB
    f. VIRTUA
    g. Other

10. Which of the following digital library software do you use in the library?
    a. GSDL
    b. D-Space
    c. E-Print
    d. None

11. Please mention the total number of PCs/workstations available to the library technical staff:
    Number of Computers/PCs..

12. Please indicate the library services available in the library (Please tick):
    a. User Education
    b. CAS
    c. SDI
    d. Indexing Services
    e. Abstracting Services
    f. Reprographic Services
    g. Translation Services
    h. Referral Service
    i. Literature Search Services

13. Is your library connected/associated with? (Please tick)
    a. DELNET
    b. INFLIBNET
    c. BONET
    d. ADINET
    e. CALIBNET
    f. MLIBNET
    g. NICNET
    h. SIRNET

14. Do you participate in any consortia for electronic journals? (Please tick)
    a. J-gate/JCCC
    b. UGC Infonet
    c. INDEST
    d. EBSCO

PART-B: INFORMATION LITERACY

1. Does your library provide Information Literacy (IL)?
   a. Yes b. No
   If yes, since when?

2. For whom does your library offer Information Literacy Programmes?
   a. Research Scholars b. Postgraduate Students
   c. Undergraduate Students d. Faculty
   e. Administrative Staff

3. How do you conduct Information Literacy Programmes, as per
   a. Department-wise b. Faculty-wise
   c. Class-wise d. Subject-wise
   e. Common for all category of users f. Other

4. Which social media platform services were used by the library? (Please tick)
   a. Facebook b. Orkut
   c. Blogs d. Twitter
   e. Worldflot f. WhatsApp
   g. Any other

5. Which Internet browser are you familiar with? (Please tick)
   a. Google Crome b. Mozilla Firefox
   c. Internet Explorer d. Opera
   e. Don't Know

6. Which Internet search engine do you use? (Please tick)
   a. Google b. Yahoo
   c. Rediff d. Bing
   e. Lycos f. Don't know
   g. Any other

7. As a librarian what is your prior agenda while organizing information literacy programmes?
   a. To attract students towards the library

b. To optimize the usage of library resources
c. To prepare students for group discussions
d. Ability to retrieve data for their assignment efficiently
e. Other

8. Does your organization have a librarian specifically assigned to work with faculty and students in the teacher education programme?

a. Yes   b. No

9. Have you changed or modified your course(s) to increase student awareness and knowledge of information literacy standards?

a. Yes
b. No

If yes...how?

c. Added lecture/discussion
d. Added new assignment
e. Modified existing assignment
f. Added test items
g. Other (please specify)

10. What barriers, if any, have you encountered when trying to incorporate information literacy standards into your courses?

a. Not enough time in the course to add extra content
b. Don't know how these standards relate to the content of my course
c. Don't have enough expertise to discuss the information literacy standards
d. Lack of institutional support
e. Lack of student interest
f. Students vary in technology expertise
g. Not part of the curriculum
h. None
i. Other

11. Please check any international literacy standards you use in your ILP

a. AASL – American Association of School Libraries (i.e. Information Power)
b. ACRL – Association of College and Research Libraries
c. ISET – International Society for Technology Education
d. Other (please specify) e. None

12. Does your library have an assessment tool to determine student information literacy competency?
    a. Yes
    b. No

    If yes, please specify

    c. Locally created objective test
    d. Objective test provided by the state, outside testing agency, or commercial provider
    e. Project-based
    f. Portfolio
    g. Demonstration of skills
    h. Other

13. Please tick the types of IL instruction your library has provided during the last one year. (Tick all that apply).
    a. Library orientation
    b. Guided library tour
    c. Introductory information skills (e.g. catalogue instruction, introduction to the library website)
    d. Advanced information skills (e.g. database training, advanced Internet searching)
    e. Research-level skills (e.g. conducting literature search and managing information, reference styles, citation management software training, scholarly publishing, etc.)

14. Please tick the topics covered in IL instruction programmes. (Tick all that apply).
    a. Introduction to library resources, services, and policies
    b. Online public access catalogue (OPAC)/library catalogue introduction
    c. Library website introduction

d. Identification of their own information needs
e. Online searching techniques
f. Use of medical databases
g. Use of search engines
h. Use of Higher Education Commission (HEC) Digital Library
i. Evaluation of information
j. Plagiarism awareness/ethical use of information
k. Copyright
l. Citation of information (referencing styles)
m. Use of citation management software (EndNote, RefWorks, etc.)
n. Scholarly publishing
o. Other topics (please specify)

15. When is IL instruction provided? (Tick all that apply).
    a. Whenever asked to do so
    b. To new session/first-time users
    c. IL is a required course for students
    d. At a specific time after the installation or acquisition of a new system or information sources
    e. Other (please specify)

16. Where do you provide IL instruction?
    a. In library training room
    b. In lecture hall outside the library
    c. In computer lab
    d. Other (please specify)

17. Which of the following methods do you use for IL instruction? (Tick all that apply).
    a. Face-to-face
    b. Workshops/seminars
    c. Online/web-based tutorials
    d. Combination of online and face to face
    e. Printed training manuals
    f. Individual instruction at the reference desk

g. Other (please specify)

18. Do you assess the effectiveness of your IL instruction session?
    a. Yes
    b. No

    If your answer is "Yes," then which of the following methods do you use for assessing effectiveness of your IL instruction session? (Tick all that apply).

    c. Quizzes
    d. Multiple choice questions
    e. Short answers
    f. Written feedback
    g. Oral feedback
    h. Assignment
    i. Assessment through practical searching in computer lab
    j. Collaborative learning exercise in class
    k. Other methods (please specify)

19. Are IL instruction programmes developed in consultation with teachers?
    a. Yes
    b. No

20. Who runs the IL instruction programmes in your institution?
    a. Librarians
    b. Faculty
    c. Both librarians and faculty in collaboration
    d. Other (please specify)

21. What, in your opinion, are the forces that hamper smooth implementation of Information Literacy Programmes in your library? (Please tick)
    a. Lack of staff
    b. Lack of trained staff for imparting user education/ information literacy programmes
    c. Lack of enthusiasm/interest in staff for conducting such a program

d. Lack of finance
e. Lack of administrative support
f. Lack of policy in this regard
g. Need for user education/information literacy programme not felt
h. Any other (please specify)

22. Do you have any suggestions and comments regarding information literacy?

....
....
....
....
....
....
....
....
....
....
....

Thank you for your time and thoughtful response.

Appendix-B

Questionnaire for Research Scholars and Postgraduate Students

QUESTIONNAIRE

4. Please tick (✓) wherever appropriate.
5. Please fill the information in the blank space.
6. You may also provide more relevant information not included in the questionnaire, in a separate sheet if required.

1. The Institute/Library
   i. Name and Address of the Library ....
   ....
   ....
   ....
   Phone No. .... Fax ....
   E-mail: ....
   ii. Head of the Library: Mr./Ms./Dr./Prof. ....
   ....
   Designation ....
   ....

2. How do you meet day-to-day information requirement?

Search	Very frequently	Fre-quently	Occa-sionally	Never
Manual searching				
Computer searching				
Internet searching				

3. Reason for using information from the library?

Purpose	Regularly	Sometimes	Rarely	Never
Research Work				
Article preparation				

Attending seminar/ workshop				
General Knowledge				
Recreational information				

4. Which format of information do you prefer?

Information Format	**Regularly**	**Sometimes**	**Rarely**	**Never**
Electronic form				
Print form				

5. From where do you get your needed information? (Please tick)
   a. Central Library
   b. From senior faculty
   c. Purchase/personal collection
   d. Use Online Resources
   e. Newspaper
   f. Television/Radio

6. Please tick (✓) the frequently used information sources (You may " more than one)

Information Sources	
Print/Electronic Journals	
Textbooks	
Reference Books	
Newsletters	
Theses/Dissertations	
Wikipedia	
E-database/e-books	

7. To find a book on the shelf in the library you need:
   (i) ISBN number .... (ii) Call number ....
   (iii) Title .... (iv) Author ....

8. Which type of computer/gadget do you have?
   a. Personal Computer b. Laptop
   c. Tablet d. Note Pad
   e. Any other

9. Which computer peripheral are you familiar with?
   a. Printer b. Scanner
   c. Mouse d. Key Board
   e. Pen Drive f. CD/VC Drive

10. Which social platform services are you familiar with? (Please tick)
    a. Facebook b. Blogs
    c. Twitter d. Worldflot
    e. WhatsApp

11. Which Internet browser are you familiar with? (Please tick)
    a. Google Crome b. Mozilla Firefox
    c. Internet Explorer d. Opera
    e. Don't know f. Any other

12. Which Internet search engine do you use? (Please tick)
    a. Google b. Yahoo
    c. Rediff d. Bing
    e. Lycos f. Don't know
    g. Any other

13. Does your library provide Information Literacy (IL)?
    a. Yes b. No
    If yes, since when?

14. Information Literacy is provided to which category of users?
    a. Research Scholars b. Post
    c. Postgraduate Students d. Undergraduate Students
    e. Faculty f. Administrative Staff

15. Is the Information Literacy Programme conducted in stages/ phases?

a. Yes b. No

If yes, please specify

16. When is the programme conducted? (Please tick)
    a. Starting of the academic year
    b. Monthly basis
    c. Somewhere in the middle of the course
    d. No fixed time
    e. Any fixed time (please specify)

17. Where is the programme conducted? (please tick)
    (i) In the library
    (ii) In the user's workplace (i.e. department)
    (iii) Any other (please specify)

18. What are the specific information literacy skills that are included in your teaching?
    a. Internet searching
    b. Evaluation of sources
    c. Use of electronic databases such as INDEST, JSTOR, EBSCO, etc.
    d. Identification of appropriate sources for information
    e. Formulation of search strategies
    f. Other (please specify)

19. Who gives training?
    a. Library staff
    b. Academic staff
    c. Both library and academic staff in collaboration
    d. Staff of e-publishers

20. Is attending Information Literacy Programmes compulsory for all users?

    a. Yes b. No

    If yes, for which category of users

21. How would you rate your Computer Literacy Skills? Please tick (✓)

Computer Skills	High	Average	Low
Print Document File			
Open & Save File			
Make a Spreadsheet			
Copy/Transfer File			
Draw Picture			
Make Power Point Presentation (PPT)			

22. Do you use the following criteria for evaluating information in different formats?

Evaluation Criteria	Yes	No
Currency		
Relevancy		
Accuracy		
Authority		

23. How would you rate your Internet Literacy Skills?

Internet Skills	High	Average	Low
How would you rate your Internet Literacy Skills?			
Attach a file to an e-mail			
Web browsing			
Copy/ download files			
Download scholarly article			
Search in Web OPAC			

24. Has Information Literacy been integrated into the curriculum of courses run by the institution?

a. Yes   b. No

If yes, please specify

25. Are any international/national standards/models of Information Literacy followed for providing Information Literacy?

    a. Yes   b. No

    If yes, please specify

26. How is Information Literacy imparted? (Please tick)

    a. Face-to-face

       Lecture

       Seminars and discussions

       Workshops

       Library tours and demonstrations

    b. On-line

       Lecture programmes

       Seminars and discussions

       Workshops

       Virtual library tours

    c. Web-based self tutorial programmes

    d. Computer-based self-tutorial programmes on CDs

    e. Printed handout

    f. Individual help at point of use

    g. Any other, please specify

27. Which of the following items are part of the Information Literacy Programme? (Please tick)

    a. Library organizational structure

    b. Library rules and regulations

    c. Importance of library and role of library staff

    d. Information sources and their peculiarities

    e. Selection of right information source

    f. Information services provided by the library

    g. Library classification

    h. Use of library catalogue

    i. Use of other retrieval tools like indexes, bibliographies, etc.

    j. Use of path finders

k. Basics of computer
l. Using computers (practical skills)
m. Basics of internet
n. Using internet (practical skills)
o. Media literacy
p. Research literacy
q. Search strategy
r. Search engines and search techniques
s. Using e-documents and databases
t. Intellectual Property Right
u. Writing references
v. Communication literacy
w. Social literacy
x. Report writing
y. Fair use and plagiarism
z. Any other, please specify)

28. Are you aware of various search techniques and strategies?
    a. Simple key words
    b. Boolean operators (AND, OR, NOT)
    c. Truncation
    d. Field search (title, author, subject, etc.)
    e. Other

29. Do you have a separate section/staff to deal with Information Literacy Programmes?
    a. Yes   b. No
    If yes, please specify
    If no, who handles the Information Literacy Programmes?

30. Which of the following best describe(s) articles published in a scholarly journal?
    a. It includes a list of references
    b. The information is written for the lay person
    c. It has been evaluated by an editorial board before publication

d. The research method used is described
e. None of the above
f. Don't know

31. Among the characteristics that are used to evaluate the quality of an Internet site one finds:
    a. The author is known in the field
    b. The date of publication is provided
    c. The site is rapidly accessible
    d. None of the above
    e. Don't know

32. Does your institution have an assessment tool to determine student Information Literacy competency?
    a. Yes   b. No

    If yes, please specify
    (i) Locally created objective test
    (ii) Objective test conducted by the institution, outside testing agency, or commercial provider
    (iii) Project based
    (iv) Portfolio
    (v) Demonstration of skills
    (vi) Other

33. Which of the following steps are taken to promote information literacy?
    a. Circulate information to departments
    b. Post information on notice board and library blogs
    c. Post information on library website
    d. Circulate brochures, pamphlets, etc.
    e. Send individual e-mails to users
    f. Involve faculty members
    g. Any other, please specify

34. How do you incorporate research/information literacy skills into your teacher education courses?
    a. Faculty provides the instruction

b. A librarian provides the instruction
c. Faculty provides links to online tutorials or supporting materials
d. The skills are taught in another course common to all teacher education students
e. A combination of two or more of the above
f. Collaborate with librarian
g. Don't incorporate it because we assume the students already have the necessary skills
h. Other

35. What barriers, if any, have you encountered when trying to incorporate information literacy standards into your courses?
    a. Not enough time in the course to add extra content
    b. Don't know how these standards relate to the content of my course
    c. Don't have enough expertise to discussion the information literacy standards
    d. Lack of institutional support
    e. Lack of student interest
    f. Students vary in technology expertise
    g. Not part of the curriculum
    h. None
    i. Other

36. If Information Literacy Programmes are not yet introduced, will they be introduced in the near future? (Please specify tentative time of introduction)

37. What, in your opinion, are the forces that hamper smooth implementation of Information Literacy Programmes in your library? (Please tick)
    a. Lack of staff
    b. Lack of trained staff for imparting user education/ information literacy programmes
    c. Lack of enthusiasm/interest in staff for conducting such a programme

d. Lack of finance
e. Lack of administrative support
f. Lack of policy in this regard
g. Need for user education/information literacy programme not felt
h. Any other (please specify)

38. Do you have any suggestions and comments regarding Information Literacy?

....
....
....
....
....
....
....
....
....
....

Thank you for your time and thoughtful response.

(Signature of respondent)
Name ....
Qualification ....

Bibliography

Abdullah, Abrizah (2008). Empowering Students in Information Literacy Practices Using a Collaborative Digital Library for School Projects. *Journal of Educational Media and Library Sciences*, Vol. 46 (1) pp. 5-29.

Abdullah, S. E. (2007). Ethical Use of Information: How University Students fare. *ICOLIS-2007*, Kuala Lumpur, pp. 319-331.

Abid, A. (2004). Information Literacy and Lifelong Learning. World Library and Information Congress. *70th IFLA General Conference and Council*. Accessed 17 June 2016 (http://www.ifla.org/IV/ifla70/papers/116-Abid.pdf).

Agosto, D.E. and Hughes-Hassell, S. (2006). Towards a Model of the Everyday Life Information Needs of Urban Teenagers, Part I: Theoretical Model. *Journal of the American Society for Information Science and Technology*, Vol. 57 (10), pp. 1394-1403.

Ajayi, N. A. (2004). Library Use and Information Seeking Behaviour of Medical Students. *Anthropologists*, Vol. 6 (3), pp. 209-213.

Alexander, O.D. (2006). Library Services for the Unemployed and the Institute for Information Literacy. *Virginia Libraries*, Vol. 52 (2), pp. 34-35.

Ali, Rosmah, Norihan Abu-Hassan (2010). Information Literacy Skills of Engineering Students. *International Journal of Research and Reviews in Applied Sciences*, Vol. 5 (3), pp. 264-270.

American Library Association (ALA) (2000). *Information Literacy Competency Standards for Higher Education*. Chicago: ALA.

American Library Association (ALA), Association of College and Research Libraries (ACRL) (1989). Presidential Committee on Information Literacy. Accessed 8 August 2016. (http://

www.ala.org/ala/mgrps/divs/acrl/publications/whitepapers/presidential.cfm)

American Library Association (ALA), Association of College and Research Libraries (2007). Information Literacy Competency Standards for Higher Education. Accessed on 7 August 2016. (www.ala.org/ala/mgrps/divs/acrl/standards/informaionliteracycompetency.cfm)

Anafo, Peter and Filson, Christopher (2014) Promoting Information Literacy Among Undergraduate Students of Ashesi University College. *Library Philosophy and Practice* (e-journal), paper 1032.

Anastasi, A. (1970). *Psychological Testing* (3rd ed.). London: The Macmillani.

Anderson, L. and Bull, S. (2014). The Creation of a University Library Outreach Programme to Develop the Information Literacy of Further Education Students: and Interactive Approach To Support Transition. *Journal of Information Literacy*, Vol. 8(1), pp. 42-57.

Andretta, S. (2005). *Information Literacy Practitioner's Guide*. Oxford: Chandos.

Anwarul, Islam and Mezbah-ul-Islam, Muhammad (2010). Community Information Services Through Public Libraries in Bangladesh: Problems and Proposals. *Library Philosophy and Practice* (e-journal). Paper 320. Accessed 2 January 2016 (http://www.digitalcommons.unl.edu/libphilprac/320).

Anwarul, Islam and Mostaq, Gausal Hoq, Kazi (2010). Community Internet Access in Rural Areas: A Study on Community Information Centres in Bangladesh. *Malaysian Journal of Library and Information Science*, Vol. 15 (2), pp. 109-124.

Anwarul, Islam and Tsuji, Keita (2010). Assessing Information Competency of Information Science Library Management Graduate Students of Dhaka University. *International Federation of Library Association and Institutions*. Vol. 36 (4), pp. 300-316.

Australian Library and Information Association (2006). Statement on Information Literacy for all Australians. Accessed on 16 July 2016. (http://alia.org.au/policies/information.literacy.html)

Behrens, S. J., Olen, S., and Machet, M.P. (1999). *Mastering Information Skills*. Pretoria: Unisa Press.

Best, J. W. (1981). *Research in Education* (4th ed.). Bombay: Prentice Hall Limited.

Bhanu, Pratap (2014). Role of Public Libraries in Community Development: A Case Study of T.S. Central State Library, Chandigarh. *International Journal of Information Dissemination and Technology*, Vol. 4 (3), pp. 224-229.

Bhardwaj, Raj Kumar (2012). Online Legal Information Systems in India: A Case Study from the Faculty of Law, University of Delhi. *Legal Information Management*, Vol. 12 (2), pp. 137-150. Accessed 18 February 2016 (http://www.journals.cambridge.org/abstrAct S147266961200357).

Bhardwaj, Raj Kumar and Madhusudhan, M. (2013). Open Access Legal Information and Their Use by Students of National Law University. *Annals of Library and Information Studies*, Vol. 60, pp. 314-319.

Bhatt, R. K. (2011). Information Literacy Models and Competencies Development Initiative in India. Accessed 2 January 2016. (http://www.uits,sla.org/chapter/cas/R%20k%Bhatt.doc)

Biradar, B. S. and Swapna, G. (2011). Information Literacy Competency: A Study of Bioscience Students of Kuvempu University. *8th International CALIBER*, 2011, Goa University, Goa, pp. 445-455.

Birch, R. (2012). *The Impact of Information Literacy Instruction on the Library Anxiety and Information Competency of Graduate Students*. Olivet: Nazarene University.

Birdsong, L. (2009). Information Literacy Training for All: More Outliers. *Searcher*, Vol. 17 (8). (http://www.infotoday.com/searcher/sep09/Nirdsong. shtml)

Blevens, C. L. (2012). Catching Up with Information Literacy Assessment Resources for Programme Evaluation. *College and Research Libraries News*, pp. 202-206.

Bob, C., Poullin, S. and Luigina, V. (1995). Evaluating Library Instruction in Academic Libraries: A Critical Review of the Literature, 1980-1993. *The Reference Librarian*, Vol. 51/52, pp. 53-71.

Boger, T. S. (2016). An Assessment of Library Instruction: Its Influence on Search Behavior of First-and Third-Year Students. *Journal of Information Literacy*, Vol. 10 (2), pp. 64-77.

Boger, T. S., Dybvik, H., Eng, A. and Norheim, E. H. (2015). The Impact of Library Information Literacy Classes on First-Year Undergraduate Students' Search Behaviour. *Journal of Information Literacy*, 9(1), pp. 34-46.

Boss, K., Angell, K. and Tewell, E. (2015). The Amazing Library Race: Tracking Student Engagement and Learning Comprehension in Library Orientations. *Journal of Information Literacy*, 9 (1), pp. 4-14.

Bradely, Cara (2013). Information Literacy Articles in Science Pedagogy Journals. *Evidence Based Library and Information Practice*, Vol. 8 (4).

Bruce C. (2008). *Informed Learning*. Chicago: Association of College and Research Libraries.

Bruce, C. (1997). *The Seven Faces of Information Literacy*. Adelaide: Auslib Press.

Bruce, C. (2000). Information Literacy Research: Dimensions of the Emerging Collective Consciousness. *Australian Academic and Research Libraries*, Vol. 31 (2), pp. 91-109.

Bundy, A. (2002). Growing the Community of the Informed: Information Literacy-A Global Issue. *Australian Academic and Research Libraries*, Vol. 33(3), pp. 125-134.

Bundy, A. (2004). *Australian and New Zealand Information Literacy Framework: Principles, Standards and Practice*. Adelaide: Australian and New Zealand Institute of Information Literacy.

Burgoyne, Mary Beth and Cornell, Kim Chuppa (2015). Beyond Embedded: Creating an Online-Learning Community Integrating Information Literacy and Composition Courses. *The Journal of Academic Librarianship*, Vol. 41(4), pp. 416-421.

Burnham, E. and Peterson, E. B. (2005). Health Information Literacy: A Library Case Study. *Library Trends*, Vol. 53 (3), pp. 422-433.

Busha, C. H. and Harter, S. P. (1980). *Research Methods in Librarianship: Techniques and Interpretation*. New York: Academics Press.

Byerly, G. A. (1999). Information Literacy Skills Models: Defining the Choices. In B. Striplings, *Learning and Libraries in an Information Age: Principles and Practice*. Englewood: Libraries Unlimited, pp. 54-82.

Canadian Library Association. Accessed 15 September 2016. (http://www.cla.ca/AM/Template.cfm?Section=Information_Literacy & Template=/CM/HTMLDisplay. cfm&Content ID=9753)

CAUL (2001). Information Literacy Standards. Accessed 5 March, 2016. (http://ilp.anu.edu.ac/infolit_standards_ 2001.htm)

Chagari, Sasikala (2005). Information Capability Building: Role of Information Literacy Programme: A Voyage of Discovery, Oslo, Norway, 14-18 August.

Chakravarty, Rupak (2008). Information Literacy in the Knowledge Society: Empowering Learners for a Better Tomorrow. *ICSSR Seminar on Trends and Strategic Issues for Libraries in Global Information Society*, Chandigarh, 18-19 March, pp.303-314.

Chu, S. K. and Law, N. (2008). The Development of Information Search Expertise of Research Students. *Journal of Librarianship and Information Science*, pp. 165-177.

CILIP. Accessed 7 February 2016. (http://www.cilip.org.uk/about/spcial-interest-group/information-literacy-group).

Click, Amanda and Petit, Joan (2010). Social Networking and Web 2.0 in Information Literacy. *The International Information and Library Review*, Vol. 42 (2), pp. 137-142.

Conteh-Morgan, M. E. (2001). Empowering ESL Students: A New Model for Information Literacy Instruction. *Research Strategies*, Vol. 18, pp. 29-38.

Crawford, John and Irving, Christine (2007). Information Literacy: The Link Between Secondary and Tertiary Education Project and its Wider Implications. *Journal of Librarianship and Information Science*, Vol. 39 (1). pp. 17-26.

Crawford, John and Irving, Christine (2009). Information Literacy in the Workplace: A Qualitative Exploratory Study. *Journal of Librarianship and Information Science*, Vol. 41(1), pp. 29-38.

Cullen, R. (2005). Empowering Patients through Health Information Literacy Training. *Library Review*, Vol. 54 (4), pp. 231-244.

Curzon, L. B. (2004). *Teaching in Further Education: An Outline of Principles and Practice*. London: Continuum.

Curzon, S. C. (2000). Developing a Programme for Information Literacy. *College and Research Libraries News*, Vol. 61, pp. 483-491.

D'Esposito, J. E., and Gardner, R. (1999). University Students' Perception of the Internet: An Exploratory Study. *The Journal of Academic Librarianship*, Vol. 25 (6), pp. 456-461.

Dalvi, Mahesh, M. (2010). Information Literacy for Effective Use of E-resources: A Study of Selected Colleges in Mumbai. In S. Srinivasaraghavan and E. Ramganesh (Eds.). *International Conference on E-resources in Higher Education: Issues, Developments, Opportunities and Challenges*, pp. 82-85. Tiruchirapalli: Bharathidasan University.

Das, Anup Kumar and Banwari Lal (2012). Information Literacy and Public Libraries in India. Accessed 23 December 2015.

(http://www.openmed.nic.in/1278/01/Information_Literacy_Public_Libraries_India.pdf).

Davis, E.L., Lundsrom, K. and Martin, P.N. (2011). Librarian Perceptions and Information Literacy Instruction Models. *Reference Services Review*. Vol. 39 (4), pp. 686-702.

Davis-Kahl, Stephanic and Payne, Lisa (2003). Teaching, Learning and Research: Linking High School Teachers to Information Literacy. *Reference Service Review*, Vol. 31(4), pp. 313-319.

De Jager, K. (1997). Library Use and Academic Achievement. *South African Journal of Library and Information Science*, Vol. 65 (1), pp. 26-30.

DeMars, C.E., Cameron, L., and Erwin, T.D. (2003). Information Literacy as Foundational: Determining Competence. *Journal of General Education*, Vol. 52 (4), pp. 253-266.

Derakhshan, Maryam (2015). Developing Information Literate Librarians: A Study of LIS Academics Pedagogical Approaches in the Development of Information Literacy Competencies. *The Journal of Academic Librarianship*, Vol. 41, pp. 777-785.

Deshpande, Neela and Shelae, Vandana (2005). Information Literacy Programme for Academic Libraries. Libraries, Information Literacy and Lifelong Learning: 51st All India Library Conference papers, Kurukshetra, December 16-18, 2005. New Delhi: Indian Library Association, pp. 265-269.

Dhanesar, S. (2006). *The Impact of Collaboration Between Faculty and Librarians to Improve Students' Information Literacy Skills at an Urban Community College*. Maryland: Morgan State University.

Diller, K. and Phelps, S. (2008). *Learning Outcomes, Portfolios, and Rubrics, Oh My! Authentic Assessment of an Information Literacy Programme*. Portal: Libraries and the Academy, Vol. 8(1), pp. 22-26.

Dixit, R. P. (1995). *Information Management in Indian Medical Libraries*. New Delhi: New Concepts.

Dold, Claudia J. (2014). Critical Information Literacy: A Model for Transdisciplinary Research in Behavioral Sciences. *The Journal of Academic Librarianship*, Vol. 40, (3-4), pp. 179-184.

Dotten, Rose (2003). The National Emphasis: Where it Counts. *School Libraries in Canada*, Vol. 23(1), pp. 15-17.

Doyle, Christiana S. (1994). *Information Literacy in an Information Society: A Concept of the Information Society*. New York: Eric

Clearing House on Information Technology, Syracuse University. Accessed 5 July 2016 (http://www.eric.ed.gov/ERICWebPortal/recordDetail?accno= ED351033)

Dunn, K. (2002). Assessing Information Literacy Skills in the California State University: A Progress Report. *Journal of Academic Librarianship*, Vol. 28 (1-2), pp. 2635.

Ebiwolate, P. B. (2010). The Use of the Library Catalogue by Undergraduate Students in Niger Delta University Library. *Library Philosophy and Practice*.

Edwards, S. L. and Bruce, C. (2002). Reflective Internet Searching: An Action Research Model. The Learning Organization, Vol. 9 (4), pp. 180-188.

Eisenberg, M. and Berkowitz. (1990). *A Big 6 Skills Overview*. Accessed 16 January 2016. (http://www.big6.com/showarticle.php?id=16).

Eisenberg, M. B. (1991). Transferability of Library Research Skills from High School to College. *School Library Media Quarterly*, Vol. 20 (*Fall*), pp. 33-42.

Eisenberg, Michael B. (2008). Information Literacy: Essential Skills for the Information Age. *DESIDOC Journal of Library and Information Technology*, Vol. 28 (2), pp. 39-47.

Emami, Maryam and Sohrab Seify (2012). Determining the Information Literacy Competence (ILC) of Faculty Members in the University of Applied Sciences and Technology. *Interdisciplinary Journals of Contemporary Research in Business*. Vol. 3 (9), pp. 1488-1495.

Emmett, A. and Emde, J. (2007). Assessing Information Literacy Skills Using ACRL Standards as Guide. *Reference Services Review*, Vol. 35 (2), pp. 210-229.

Eskola, Eeva-Liisa (2005). Information Literacy of Medical Students Studying in the Problem-Based and Traditional Curriculum. *Information Research*, Vol. 10 (2).

Evangelista-Marquez, Jose Luis and Tarango, Javier (2013). Critical Pedagogy and Information Literacy in Higher Education: A Theoretical Approach. *International Journal of Information Research*, Vol. 3 (1), September, 2013. pp. 1-14.

Exner, Nina (2014). Research Information Literacy: Addressing Researchers' Needs. *The Journal of Academic Librarianship*, Vol. 40 (5), pp. 460-466.

Fain, Margaret (2011). Assessing Information Literacy Skills Development in First Year Students: A Multi-Year Study. *The Journal of Academic Librarianship*, Vol. 37 (2). pp. 109-119.

Ferguson, Jessame E. (2006). A baseline Information Literacy Assessment of Biology Students. *Reference & User Services Quarterly*, Vol. 46 (2), pp. 61-71.

Ferguson, Jessame E. Teresa Y. Neely and Kathryn, Sullivan (2006). A Basement Information Literacy of Biology Students. *Reference & User Services Quarterly*, Vol. 46 (2), pp. 67-71.

Fjallbrant, Nancy (2002). Information Literacy for Scientists and Engineers: Experience of EDUCATE-DEDICATE. *Programme: Electronic Library and Information System*, Vol. 34 (3), pp. 257-268.

Fjallbrant, Nancy and Malley (1984). *User Education Libraries*. London: Department of Educational Skills.

Foggett, Tracy (2003). Information Literacy at the Primary School Level. *Australian Library Journal*, Vol. 52 (1), pp. 55-63.

Foo, Schubert (2013). Information Literacy Skills of Humanities, Arts, and Social Science Tertiary Students in Singapore. *Reference & User Services Quarterly*, Vol. 53, No. 1, pp. 40-50.

Ford, Barban, J. (1991). Information Literacy. *College and Research Libraries*, Vol. 52 (4), pp. 313-314.

Forster, M. (2015). Refining the Definition of Information Literacy: The Experience of Contextual Knowledge Creation. *Journal of Information Literacy*, 9 (1), pp. 62-73.

Fosmire, Michael (2012). Information Literacy and Engineering Design: Developing an Integrated Conceptual Model. *IFLA*, Vol. 38(1), pp. 47-52

Foster, A. E. (2006). Information Literacy for the Information Profession: Experience from Aberystwyth. *ASLIB Proceedings*, Vol. 58 (6), pp. 488-501.

Foster, S. (1993). Information Literacy: Some Misgivings. *American Libraries*, Vol. 24 (4), pp. 344-346.

Gadd, Elizabeth, Baldwin, Andrew and Norris, Michael (2010). The Citation Behaviour of Civil Engineering Students. *Journal of Information Literacy*, Vol. 4(2), pp. 37-49.

Garland, K. (1995). The Information Search Process: A Study Elements Associated with Meaningful Research Tasks. *School Libraries Worldwide*, Vol. (1), pp. 41-53.

Gatten, J. N. (2004). Student Psychosocial and Cognitive Development: Theory to Practice in Academic Libraries. *Reference Services Review*. Vol. 32 (2), pp. 157-163.

Ghosh, S. B. and Das, A. K. (2006) Information Literacy Initiatives in India with Special Reference to Emerging Knowledge Economy. *Proceedings* of *International Conference on Information Literacy,* Kuala Lumpur. June 14-15, pp. 1-11.

Ghulam Murtaza, Rafique (2014). Information Literacy Skills of Faculty Members: A Study of the University of Lahore, Pakistan. *Library Philosophy and Practice*. Paper 1072.

Gipps, C. V. (1994). *Beyond Testing: Towards a Theory of Educational Assessment*. London: Falmer.

Goldstein, Stephane (2012). A Partnership Approach to Promoting Information Literacy for Higher Education Research. *Liber Quarterly,* Vol. 21 (2).

Gordon, Carol A. (2009). An Emerging Theory for Evidence Based Information Literacy Instruction in School Libraries. *Evidence Based Library and Information Practice,* Vol. 4(2). pp. 56-77.

Grafstein, A. (2002). A Discipline Based Approach to Information Literacy. *Journal of Academic Librarianship,* Vol. 28 (4), pp. 194-205.

Grassian, E. S. and Kaplowitz, J. R. (2001). *Information Literacy Instruction*. New York: Neal-Scheman.

Grassian, F. (2004). Building on Bibliographic Instruction. *American Libraries,* Vol. 51-53.

Gross, M. and Latham, D. (2007). Attaining Information Literacy: An Investigation of the Relationship between Skill Level, Self Estimates of Skill, and Library Anxiety. *Library and Information Science Research,* Vol. 29 (3), pp. 332-353.

Guven, M. (2008). Information Literacy: Learning to Learn and Teacher Training. *Electronic Journal of Social Sciences.*

Haberle, N. (2001). *Developing an Evaluative Framework for Information Literacy Interventions*. Cape Town: Cape Technikon.

Hadimani, Manjunath B. and Rajgoli, Iqbalahmad U. (2010). Assessing Information Literacy Competence Among the Undergraduate Students of the College of Agriculture, Raichur: A Case Study. *DESIDOC Journal of Library & Information Technology*. Vol. 30 (2), pp. 70-78.

Haneefa, Mohamed K. and Shukkoor, C. K. Abdul (2010). Information and Communication Technology Among Library Professionals in Calicut University, Kerala. *DESIDOC Journal of Library and Information Technology*. Vol. 30 (6), pp. 55-63.

Harada, V. H. (2002). Personalizing the Information Search Process: A Case Study of Journal Writing with Elementary-Age Students. *School Library Media Research*, Vol. 5.

Harrington, M. R. (2009). Information Literacy and Research Intensive Graduate Students: Enhancing the Role of Research Librarians. *Behavioural and Social Sciences Librarian*, Vol. 28 (4), pp. 179-201.

Head, Alison J. (2013). Project Information Literacy: What Can be Learned About the Information Seeking Behavior of Today's College Students? *Indianpolis*, pp. 472-482.

Hernon, P. and Dugan, R. (2002). *An Action Plan for Outcomes Assessment in Your Library*. Chicago: ALA.

Herring, J. (2011). Year 7 Students, Information Literacy and Transfer: A Grounded Theory. *School Library Research*, Vol. 15.

Hodgens, C., Sendall, M., and Evans, L. (2012). Postgraduate Health Promotion Students Assess Their Information Literacy. *Reference Services Review*, Vol. 40 (3), pp. 408-422.

Hollister, Christopher (2005). Bringing Information Literacy to Career Services. *Reference Services Review*, Vol. 33 (1), pp. 104-111.

Hopkins, F.L. (1982). A Century of Bibliographic Instruction: The Historic Claim to Professional and Academic Legitimacy. *College and Research Libraries*, pp. 192-198.

Hsieh, Ma Lei and Dawson, Patricia A. (2014). Four Pedagogical Approaches in Helping Students Learn Information Literacy Skills. *The Journal of Academic Librarianship*, Vol. 40 (3-4), pp. 234-246.

Hughes, Sandra (2003). The Big 6: A Strategy for Student Research. *School Libraries in Canada*, Vol. 22 (4), pp. 28-29.

Hurst, Leslie (2003). The Special Library on Campus: A Model for Library Orientations Aimed at Academic Administration, Faculty and Support Staff. *Community and College Libraries*, Vol. 11 (2), pp. 31-64.

Huvila, Isto (2011). The Complete Information Literacy? Unforgetting Creation and Organization Of Information. *Journal of Librarianship and Information Science*, Vol. 43 (4). pp. 237-245.

Inskip, Charles (2015). Information Literacy in LIS Education: Exploring the Student View. *Journal of Information Literacy*, Vol. 9(2), pp. 94-110.

Intan, A. M. and Foo, S. (2008). Information Literacy Education: Application of Mediated Learning and Multiple Intelligences. *Library and Information Science Research*, Vol. 30 (3), pp. 195-206.

Irving, A. (1985). *Study and Information Skills Across the Curriculum*. London: Heinemann.

Islam, Anwarul and Chowdhury, Salma (2010). Assessing Information Competency of ISLM Graduate Students of Dhaka University: An Analysis. *Library Herald*, Vol. 48 (4), pp. 320-344.

Islam, Mohammed Anwarul and Tsuji, Keita (2010). Assessing Information Literacy Competency of Information Science and Library Management Graduate Students of Dhaka University. *IFLA Journal*, 36(4), pp. 300-316.

Jacobson, T. E. and Xu, L. (2004). *Motivating Students in Information Literacy Classes*. New York: Neal Schuman.

Jayaprakash and Gupta, V. Yugender (2005). Information Literacy: Need to Promote the Use of Digital Information Services in the Modern Era. *51st All India Library Conference of Indian Library Association on Libraries, Information Literacy and Lifelong Learning*. Kurukshetra, pp. 292-301.

Jeyaraman, R. Srinivasaraghavan, S. and Duraisamy, M. (2011). Awareness on Information Literacy of the Respondents in Tamil Nadu Agricultural University, India: A Discriminate Function Analysis Approach. *Asian Journal of Information Science and Technology*, Vol. 1 (1), pp. 42-46.

Jinadu, Iliasu and Kaur, Kiran (2014). Information Literacy at the Workplace: A Suggested Model for a Developing Country. *Libri*, Vol. 64(1), pp. 61-74.

Jiyane, Glenrose Velile and Onyancha, Omwoyo Bosire (2010). Information Literacy Education and Instruction in Academic Libraries and LIS Schools in Institutions of Higher Education in South Africa. *South Africa Journal of Libraries and Information Science*, Vol. 76 (1), 2010. pp. 11-23.

Johnson, H. (2001). Information Skills, Information Literacy. *Library Association Record*, Vol. 103 (12), pp. 752-753.

Joshi, Manoj K. and Sharma, Sanjeev (2005). Need for Information Literacy Education in Kurukshetra University. Libraries, Information Literacy and Lifelong Learning: 51st All India Library Conference Papers, Kurukshetra, December 16-18, 2005. New Delhi: Indian Library Association. pp. 249-258.

Joshi, Manoj Kumar and Sharma, Sanjeev (2009). Students Use of Various Information Sources and Need for Information Literacy in Kurukshetra University. *Library Herald*, Vol. 47 (1), pp. 46-59.

Kargbo, J. A. (2010). Undergraduate Students' Problems with Citing References. *Reference Librarian*, Vol. 51 (3), pp. 222-236.

Karim, S. A (1993). Status of Health Science Libraries and Librarians in India. *MLAI National Convention and Workshop on Information Technology and Health Science Libraries*, pp. 143-144.

Karisiddappa, C. R. and Kavita, H. C. (2004). Information Literacy as a Means of Information Empowerment. *University News*, Vol. 42 (49), pp. 11-15.

Karisiddappa, C. R. and Rajgoli, Iqbalahmad U. (2008). In Search of Information Literacy Programme and Practices: Survey of Selected Institutions at Bangalore. *DESIDOC Journal of Library and Information Technology*. Vol. 28 (2), pp. 28-38.

Katz, I. R. (2007). Testing Information Literacy in Digital Environments: ETS skills Assessment. *Information Technology and Libraries*, Vol. 26, pp. 3-12.

Kaul, L. (2007). *Methodology of Educational Research*. New Delhi: Vikas Publishing.

Kerr, P. (2010) *Conceptions and Practice of Information Literacy in Academic Libraries: Espoused Theories and Theories in Use*. New Brunswick: New Jersey.

Kim, Sung Un and Shumaker, David (2015). Student, Librarian, and Instructor Perceptions of Information Literacy Instruction and Skills in a First Year Experience Programme: A Case Study. *The Journal of Academic Librarianship*, Vol. 41(4), pp. 449-456.

Kirton, J. and Barham, L. (2005). Information Literacy in the Workplace. *Australian Library Journal*, Vol. 54 (4), pp. 365-376.

Kirton, J. and Barham, L. (2008). Understanding and Practice of Information Literacy in Australian Government Libraries. *Australian Library Journal*, Vol. 57 (3), pp. 237-256.

Kishore, Avineni and M. Padmaja (2013). Information Literacy Skills of the Postgraduate Students Towards the Use of Electronic Information Resources: A Case Study of SVIMS Library, Tirupati. *Libraries in the Changing Dimensions of Digital Technology*, pp. 204-212.

Knight, L. A. (2002). The Role of Assessment in Library User Education. *Reference Services Review*, Vol. 30 (1), pp. 15-24.

Kolb, D. A. (1984). *Experimental Learning: Experience as the Source of Learning and Development*. New Jersey: Prentice Hall.

Koneru, Indira (2010). ADDIE: Designing Web-Enabled Information Literacy Instructional Modules. *DESIDOC Journal of Library and Information Technology*, Vol. 30 (3), pp. 23-34.

Korobili, Stella, Aphrodite Malliari and George N. Christodoulou (2009). Assessing Information Literacy Skills in the Technological Education Institute of Thessaloniki, Greece. *Reference Service Review*, Vol. 37 (3), pp. 340-354.

Kothari, C. R. (2004). Research Methodology: Methods and Techniques, 2nd ed. New Delhi: New Age International.

Kuan-Nien, C. and Pei-Chun, L. (2011). Information Literacy in University Library User Education. *Aslib Proceedings*, Vol. 64 (4), pp. 399-418.

Kuffalikar, Chitra Rekha and Rajyalakshmi, D. (2006). Opening the Gateways of Knowledge Through E-Information Literacy: A New Vision. *4th International Convention CALIBER-2006*, 2-4 February, pp. 265-276.

Kuhlthau, C. (1999). Literacy and Learning for the Information Age. In B. Stripling. *Learning and Libraries in an Information Age: Principles and Practice*. Littleton: Libraries Unlimited.

Kumbar, B.D. and Lamani, Manohar B. (2014). Rural Library as Community Information Centre: A study of Karnataka State. *E-Library Science Research Journal*, Vol. 2 (11), pp. 1-5.

Kurbanoglu, S.E. (2006). Developing the Information Literacy Self-Efficacy Scale. *Journal of Documentation*, Vol. 62 (6), pp. 730-743.

Kyung-Sun, K. and Sei-Ching Joanna, S. (2011). Selecting Quality Sources: Bridging the Gap between the Perception and Use of Information Sources. *Journal of Information Science*, Vol. 37 (2), pp. 178-188.

Lai, Horng-Ji (2011). Information Literacy Training in Public Libraries: A Case Study from Canada. *Educational Technology & Society*, Vol. 14 (2), pp. 81-88

Larkin, J. E. and Pines, H. (2005). Developing Information Literacy and Research Skills in Introductory Psychology: A Case Study. *The Journal of Academic Librarianship*, Vol. 31 (1), pp. 40-45.

Lata, Suman and Sharma, Sanjeev (2012). Information Literacy Among Public Library Users With Special Reference to the T. S. Central State Library, *Chandigarh. International Journal of Information Research*, Vol. 2 No. 1, September 2012. pp. 45-60.

Lau, J. (2006). Guidelines on Information Literacy for Lifelong Learning: Final Draft. Accessed 13 November 2015. (htt:// www.ifla.org/VII/s42/pub/IL-Guidelines2006.pdf)

Laverty, C. (2008). The Challenge of Information Seeking: How Children Engage in Library Work. *Feliciter*, Vol . 48 (5), pp. 226-228.

Li, W. (2011). An Information Literacy Integration Model and its Application in Higher Education. *Reference Services Review*, pp. 703-720.

Lloyd, A. (2003). Information Literacy: The Meta-Competency of the Knowledge Economy? An Exploratory Paper. *Journal of Librarianship and Information Science*, Vol. 35 (2), pp. 87-92.

Lloyd, A. (2009). Information Practice: Information Experiences of Ambulance Officers in Training and On Road Practice. *Journal of Documentation*, Vol. 65 (3), pp. 396-419.

Lloyd, A. and Williamson, K. (2008). Towards an Understanding of Information Literacy in Context: Implications for Research. *Journal of Librarianship and Information Science*, Vol. 40 (1), pp. 3-12.

Lopez, C. L. (2002). Assessment of Student Learning: Challenges and Strategies. *Journal of Academic Librarianship*, Vol. 28 (6), pp. 356-367.

Lorenzen, M. (2001). A Brief History of Library Instruction in the United States of America. *Illinois Libraries*, pp. 8-18.

Lupton. M. (2008). Information Literacy and Learning. Adelaide: Auslib Press.

Lyn, C.W. and Lottridge, S.M. (2007). The Development and Validation of the Information Literacy Test. *College and Research Libraries*, Vol. 68, pp. 62-78.

Macauley, Peter and Green, Rosemary (2009) Can Our Relationships be Reconceptualized? Librarians, Information Literacy, and Doctoral Learners. *Journal of Education for Library and Information Science*,Vol. 50, No. 2, Spring, 2009, pp. 68-78.

Mackey, T.P. and Jacobson, T.E. (2011). Reframing Information Literacy as Metaliteracy. *College and Research Libraries*, Vol. 72 (1), pp. 62-78.

Macmillan, M. and Mackenzie, A. (2012). Strategies for Integrating Information Literacy and Academic Literacy: Helping

Undergraduate Students Make the Most of Scholarly Articles. *Library Management*, Vol. 8 (9), pp. 525-535.

Madhusoodanan, C. and Baradol, A. K. (2011). Information Literacy Competency Among the Post Graduate Students: A Case Study. *International Journal of Information Research*, Vol.1 No. 1, September, 2011. pp. 1-12.

Madhusudhan, M. (2012). Information Literacy Programmes in Select University Libraries in Delhi: A Study. *Journal of Indian Library Association*, Vol. 48 (4), pp. 5-19.

Mahadevamurthy, M., Adithya Kumara and Selvaraja, A. (2012). Information Literacy Skills Among Users of City Central Library, Mysore: A Study. *Re-inventing and Re-structuring of the Public Library System in India* (pp. 238-246). Bangalore: Karnataka State SC/ST Library Professional Association.

Maharana, Bulu and Mishra, Champeswar (2009). A Survey of Digital Information Literacy of Faculty at Sambalpur University. *Library Philosophy and Practice*. Accessed 14 April 2016. (http://digitalcommons.unl.edu/libphilprac/144).

Majid, Shaheen and Abazova, Alfia Fanilievna. Computer Literacy and Use of Electronic Information Sources by Academics: A Case Study of International Islamic University Malaysia. *Asian Libraries*, Vol. 8 (4), pp. 100-111.

Malhan, I.V.(2009). Providing Information User Communities for the Knowledge Society by Imparting Information Literacy. *SALIS Journal of Library and Information Science*, Vol. 1 (1), pp. 14-18.

Marais, J. J. (1994). Information Literacy and Quality of Life. *Free State Libraries*, pp. 13-19.

Marchionini, G. (1997). *Information Seeking in Electronic Environments*. Cambridge: Cambridge University.

Markauskaite, Lina (2006). Towards an Integrated Analytical Framework of Information and Communications Technology Literacy: From Intended to Implemented and Achieved Dimensions. *Information Research*, Vol. 11 (3).

Mattheos, N.M., Schittek, Janda (2005). A Comparative Evaluation of Computer Literacy Amongst Dental Educators and Students. *European Journal of Dental Education*, Vol. 9 (1), pp. 32-36.

Maughan, Patricia Davitt (2001). Assessing Information Literacy Among Undergraduates: A Discussion of the Literature and the

University of California-Berkeley Assessment Experience. *College ad Research Libraries*, pp. 71-85.

Maybee, Clarence (2015). It's in the Syllabus': Identifying Information Literacy and Data Information Literacy Opportunities Using a Grounded Theory Approach. *The Journal of Academic Librarianship*, Vol. 41(4), pp. 369-376.

Mckinney, Pamela (2014). Information Literacy and Inquiry-Based Learning: Evaluation of a Five-Year Programme of Curriculum Development. *Journal of Librarianship and Information Science*, Vol. 46 (2), pp. 148-166.

McNicol, Sarah (2015). Modelling Information Literacy for Classrooms of the Future. *Journal of Librarianship and Information Science*, Vol. 47 (4), pp. 303-313.

Md. Zahid, H. S. (2011). Information Literacy Competency of Freshman Business Students of a Private University in Bangladesh. *Library Review*, Vol. 60 (9), pp. 762-772.

Meegen, Ana Van and Limpens, Imke (2010). How Serious Do We Need to be Improving Information Literacy Skills Through Gaming and Interactive Elements. *LIBER Quarterly: The Journal of European Research Libraries*, Vol. 20(2).

Mishra, R. N. and Mishra C. (2010). Relevance of Information Literacy in Digital Environment. *Journal of Emerging Trends in Computing and Information Science*, Vol. 1 (1), pp. 48-54.

Mishra, R.N. and Mishra, C. (2010). Relevance of Information Literacy in Digital Environment. *Journal of Emerging Trends in Computing and Information Sciences*, Vol. 1 (1), pp. 48-54.

Mnkeni-Saurombe, Nampombe (2014). Information Literacy: A Cornerstone for Open Distance Learning at the University of South Africa. *Journal of Librarianship and Information Science*, Vol. 47 (2), pp. 156-165.

Moghaddaszadeh, Hassan and Nikam, Khaiser (2012). Attitude of Faculty Members and Research Scholars Towards Information Literacy: A Study of Bangalore University, Bangalore, India. *International Journal of Information Dissemination and Technology*, Vol. 2 (1), pp. 12-17.

Mukesh Kumar and Singla, Nareshlata (2012). Role of Legal Fraternity in Imparting Legal Literacy: A Study in India Context. *International Journal of Physical and Social Sciences*, Vol. 2(3).

Mullins, Kimberly (2014). Good IDEA: Instructional Design Model for Integrating Information Literacy, Vol. 40, pp. 339-349.

Nagaraju, K. and Roja, M. (2014). Information Literacy Assessment of Students in ATREYA Ayurvedic Medical College & Research Centre, Doddaballapur, Karnataka. *Journal of Advances in Library and Information Science*, Vol. 3 (2), pp. 110-115.

Naidoo, Segarani and Raju, Jaya (2012). Impact of the Digital Divide on Information Literacy Training in a Higher Education Context. *South Asian Journal of Library and Information Science*. Vol. 78 (1), pp. 34-44.

Nanda, Archita and Ramesh, D.B. (2012). Assessment of Information and Communication Technology (ICT) Literacy Among Teachers and Practitioners in the Field of Disability. *International Journal of Information Dissemination and Technology*, Vol. 2 (1), pp. 54-61.

Nazari, Maryam (2011). A Contextual Model of Information Literacy. *Journal of Information Science*, Vol. 37(4). pp. 345-359.

Nielsen, Bo Gerner and Borlund, Pia (2011). Information Literacy, Learning, and the Public Library: A Study of Danish High School Students. *Journal of Librarianship and Information Science*, Vol. 43(2). pp. 106-119.

Nierenberg, E. and Fjeldbu, Q. G. (2015). How Much Do First-Year Undergraduate Students in Norway Know About Information Literacy? *Journal of Information Literacy*, 9(1), pp. 15-33.

Norsrat, Riahinia. Determining the Information Literacy Competency of M.A. Students in Tarbiat Moallem University, Iran. *Library Herald*, Vol. 50 (1), pp. 15-22.

Nutbeam, D. (2008). The Evolving Concept of Health Literacy. *Social Science and Medicine*, Vol. 67, pp. 2072-2078.

O'Sullivan, C. (2002). Is Information Literacy Relevant in the Real World? *Reference Services Review*, Vol. 30(1), pp. 7-14.

Oakleaf, M. (2009). The Information Literacy Instruction Assessment Cycle: A Guide for Increasing Student Learning and Improving Librarian Instructional Skills. *Journal of Documentation*, Vol. 65 (4), pp. 539-560.

Oakleaf, Megan (2014). A Roadmap for Assessing Student Learning Using the New Framework for Information Literacy for Higher Education. *The Journal of Academic Librarianship*, Vol. 40 (6), pp. 510-514.

Omar, Abbas Mohamed (2014). Information Literacy in Zanzibar Universities: Current Situation and the Way Forward. *IFLA Journal*, Vol. 40(4), pp. 280-288.

Owusu-Ansah, E. K. (2004). Information Literacy and the Academic Library: A Critical Look at a Concept and the Controversies Surrounding It. *Journal of Academic Librarianship*, pp. 219-230.

Owusu-Ansah, E.K. (2005). Debating Definitions of Information Literacy: Enough is Enough! *Library Review*, Vol. 54 (6), pp. 366-374.

Patridge, H. (2008). Community and Workplace Information Literacy: Guest Editorial. *Australian Library Journal*, Vol. 57 (3), pp. 20-210.

Patridge, H., Bruce, C. and Tilley, C. (2008). Community Information Literacy: Developing an Australian Research Agenda. *Libri*, Vol. 58, pp. 110-122.

Patterson, A. (2009). A Needs Analysis for Information Literacy Provision for Research: A Case Study in University College Dublin. *Journal of Information Literacy*, Vol. 3 (1), pp. 5-18.

Pausch, L.M. and Popp, M.P. (1997). Assessment of Information Literacy: Lessons from the Higher Education Assessment Movement. Accessed 23 October,2015. (http://www.ala.org/acrl/publications/whitepapers/nashville/pauschpopp)

Pham, H. (2011). Theory Based Instructional Models Applied in Classroom Contexts. *Literacy Information and Computer Education Journal*, Vol. 2(2), pp. 406-415.

Pinto, Maria (2011). An approach to the Internal Facet of Information Literacy Using the IL-HUMASS Survey. *The Journal of Academic Librarianship*, Vol. 37 (2). pp. 120-129.

Pinto, Maria and Sales, Dora (2015). Uncovering Information Literacy's Disciplinary Differences Through Students' Attitudes: An Empirical Study. *Journal of Librarianship and Information Science*, Vol. 47 (3), pp. 204-215.

Radcliff, C. J., Jensen, M. L., Salem, J. A., Burhanna, K. J. and Gedeon, J. A. (2007). *A Practical Guide to Information Literacy Assessment for Academic Librarians*. Westport CT: Libraries Unlimited.

Rader, H. (1990). Information Literacy: A Revolution in the Library, *RQ*, Vol. 31, pp. 25-29.

Rajalakshmi, P. M. (2007). Towards an Information Literate Society. *Indian Journal of Library and Society*, Vol. 20 (1), pp.10-19.

Ramesh, C. (2008). Information Literacy. Need for an Urgent Action in India: A Strategic Approach. *DESIDOC Journal of Library and Information Technology*, Vol. 28 (2), pp. 66-72.

Rao, A. S. and Nagar, B. R (2005). Information Literacy: Its Impact on Teaching and Learning in 21st Century. Libraries, Information Literacy and Lifelong Learning: 51st All India Library Conference Papers, Kurukshetra, December 16-18, 2005. New Delhi: Indian Library Association. pp. 237-248.

Ratteray, O. (2002). Information Literacy in Self Study and Accreditations. *Journal of Academic Librarianship*, Vol. 28 (6), pp. 368-376.

Rockman, I. F. (2003). Information Literacy, a Worldwide Priority for the Twenty-First Century. Reference Services Review. *Journal of Further and Higher Education*, Vol. 29 (4), pp. 321-330.

Rockman, I.F. (2004). *Integrating Information Literacy into the Higher Education Curriculum*. San Francisco: Jossey-Bass.

Rowntree, D. (1987). *Assessing Students: How Shall We Know Them?* London: Kogan Page.

Rychen, D.S. and Salganik, L.H. (2005). The Definition and Selection of Key Competencies: Executive Summary. Accessed 11 June 2016. (http://oecd.org/dataoecd/47/61).

Sajjad Ur Rahmanand Alfaresi, Sumayyah. (2009). Information Literacy Skills Among Female Students in Kuwaiti High School. *Library Review*, Vol. 58 (8), pp. 607-616.

Sardesai, Kshipra (2005). Information Literacy. Libraries, Information Literacy and Lifelong Learning: 51st All India Library Conference Papers, Kurukshetra, December 16-18, 2005. New Delhi: Indian Library Association, pp. 302-312.

Sasikala, C. and Dhanraju, V. (2011). Assessment of Information Literacy Skills Among Science Students of Andhra University. *Library Philosophy and Practice*. Accessed 6 September 2016. (http://unllib.unl.edu/LPP/.)

Sasikala, C. and Dhanraju, V. (2011). Assessment of Information Literacy Skills Among Science Students of Andhra University. *Library Philosophy and Practice* (e-journal).

Satish, Kanamadi and Vishakha, Vichare (2006). Information Literacy Programmes for Social Scientists: A Tool for Harnessing E-resources. *SRELS Journal of Information Management*, Vol. 43 (3), pp. 283-293.

Saunders, L. (2009). The Future of Information Literacy in Academic Libraries: A Delphi Study. Portal: Libraries and the Academy, Vol. 9(1), pp. 99-114.

Saunders, L. (2012). Faculty Knowledge of Information Literacy Standard has an Impact in the Classroom. *Journal of Academic Librarianship*, Vol. 38 (4), pp. 226-236.

Savolainen, Reijo and Talja, Sanna (2005). Information Literacy as Socio Technical Practice. *The Library Quarterly*, Vol. 75 (3), pp. 329-345.

Sayed, Y. and Jager, K, (1997). Towards an Investigation of Information Literacy of South African Students. *South African Journal of Library and Information Science*, Vol. 65 (1), pp. 5-13.

Scharf, D. E. (2007). Direct Assessment of Information Literacy Using Writing Portfolios. *Journal of Academic Librarianship*, Vol. 33 (4), pp. 462-477.

Secker, J. (2004). E-learning and Information Literacy. In J. Secker, *Electronic Resources in the Virtual Learning Environment: A Guide for Librarianship*. Oxford: Chandos, pp-53-74

Secker, J. and Rowena, M (2011). Evaluating M1512: An Information Literacy Course for Ph.D. Students. *Library Review*, Vol. 60 (2), pp. 96-107.

Seiler, Vilve (2012). How to Fit Teaching of Information Literacy in With Students' Needs: An On-Line Credit Course Model From the University of Tartu Library. *Liber Quarterly*, Volume 22 (1), pp. 42-63.

Seneviratne, T. M. and Wickramasinghe (2010). Information Literacy Skills of Undergraduates of University of Moratuwa. *Journal of the University Librarians Association of Sri Lanka*, Vol. 14 (1), pp. 15-30.

Senlson, P. and Stillwell, L. (2001). Transforming Bibliographic Instruction Activities into an Information Literacy Programme: Challenges and Opportunities. *ACRL Tenth National Conference*. Denver: ACRL, pp. 226-230.

Sevukan, R. and Brahma, Sanjeeb Kumar (2011). Digital Information Literacy Among Postgraduate Students and Research Scholars of Pondicherry University: A Study. *NIFT-ICLM: User Empowerment Through Digital Technologies*, pp. 195-204.

Shapiro, J. and Hughes, J. K. (1996). Information Literacy as a Liberal Art: Enlightenment Proposals for a New Curriculum.

EDUCOM Review, pp. 31-35. Accessed 8 May 2016 (http://www.educause.edu)

Sharma, Yogita (2010). Information Literacy in Indian Agricultural Universities: A Study of Punjab Agricultural Universities. *Library Herald*, Vol. 48 (4), pp. 345-357.

Shenton, Andrew K. (2009). *IFLA Journal*, Vol. 35 (3), pp. 226-231

Shenton, Andrew K. (2011). Uniting Information Literacy Promotion and Reader Development in Schools: Two Forms Of Library-Based Intervention. *IFLA Journal*, Vol. 37(1), pp. 62-68.

Shenton, Andrew K. and Hay-Gibson, Naomi(2011). Information Behavior and Information Literacy: The Ultimate In Transdisciplinary Phenomena. *Journal of Librarianship and Information Science*, Vol. 43(3). pp. 166-175.

Shinew, D. M. and Walter, S. (2003). *Information Literacy for Educators Professional Knowledge for an Information Age*. New York: Haworth Press.

Siddike, Abul Kalam. Exploring Digital Literacy Competencies Among the Library and Information Professionals of Bangladesh: Problems and Recommendations. *55th ILA National Conference.*

Sieberhagen, Anee and Cloete, Linda (2012). The Evaluation of Digital Information Literacy Programme. *South Asian Journal of Library and Information Science*, Special issue, pp. 20-41.

Singh, Jagtar (2008). Sense Making: Information Literacy for Life Long Learning and Knowledge Management. *DESIDOC Journal of Library and Information Technology*, Vol. 28 (2), pp. 13-17.

Singh, Yogesh Kumar (2005). *Research Methodology*. New Delhi: A.P.H. Publishing Corporation.

Snavely, L. and Cooper, N. (1997). The Information Literacy Debate. *Journal of Academic Librarianship*, Vol. 23 (1), pp. 9-20.

Spink, A., Bateman, J. and Jansen, B. (1998). Searching Heterogeneous Collections on the Web: Behaviour of Excited Users. *Information Research.* Accesses 11 March, 2017 (http://www.informationr.net/ir/4)

Spiranec, S. and Zorica, M.B. (2010). Information Literacy 2.0: Hype or Discourse Refinement? *Journal of Documentation*, Vol. 66 (1), pp. 140-153.

Spitzer, K., Eisenberg, M. and Lowe, C. (1998). *Information Literacy: Essential Skills for the Information Age*. Syracuse: ERIC Clearing House on Information and Technology.

Stec, E. (2004). *Guidelines for Information Literacy Assessment*. Accessed 2 June 2016 (http://www.ifla.org/files/assests/information-literacy/publications/il-guidelines-2004-en.pdf)

Stella, Korobili (2011). A Paradigm Of Information Literacy for Greek High School Teachers. *Journal of Librarianship and Information Science*, Vol. 43 (2). pp. 78-87.

Sun, P. (2002). Information Literacy in Chinese Higher Education. *Library Trends*. Vol. 51 (2), pp. 210-218.

Swanson, T. (2004). A Radical Step: implementing a Critical Information Literacy Model. *Libraries and Academy*, Vol. 4 (2), pp. 259-278.

Syamalamba, Rani (2011) Information Literacy Programme for Undergraduate Students. *International Journal of Digital Library Services*, Vol. 1 (1), pp. 49-90

Tanner, Annelle Pierce, Susan (2004). Readiness for Evidence Based Practice: Information Literacy Needs of Nurses in the United States. *EDINFO*, pp. 936-940.

Taylor, R. S. (1979). Reminiscing About the Future. *Library Journal*, Vol. 104, pp. 1871-1875.

Tewell, Eamon C. (2013). Full-Time Faculty View Information Literacy as Important But are Unlikely to Incorporate it into Their Teaching. *Evidence Based Library and Information Practice*, Vol. 8(1), pp. 84-86.

Thansukodi, S. (2010). Information Literacy in India: An Overview. *India Journal of Library and Information Science*, Vol. 4 (3), pp. 205-231.

Thapa, Neelam (2014). Information Literacy: Key to Lifelong Learning. Vol. 5(1), pp. 7-12.

Thomas, N. P. (1999). *Information Literacy and Information Skills Instruction: Applying Research to Practice in the School Library Media Centre*. Englewood: Libraries Unlimited.

Tirado, Alejandro Uribe (2012). Information Literacy Competency Standards for Higher Education and Their Correlation With the Cycle of Knowledge Generation. *LIBER Quarterly*, Vol. 22 (3), pp. 213-239.

Tolar, Burton, V. and Chadwick, S. A. (2000). Investigating the Practices of Student Researchers: Patterns of Use and Criteria for Use of Internet and Library Sources. *Computers and Composition*, Vol. 17 (3), pp. 309-328.

Torras, Maria-Carme (2009). *Information Literacy Education: A Process Approach: Professionalizing the Pedagogical Role of Academic Libraries*. Oxford: Chandos Publishing.

Tucker, B. and Palmer, S. (2004). *Integration of Informaology Education Literacy Training into Engineering and Technology Education*. Accessed 7 July 2016 (http://www.vala.org.au/vala2004/2004pdfs/36TucPal.pdf)

Twait, M. (2005). Undergraduate Students' Source Selection Criteria: A Qualitative Study. *The Journal of Academic Librarianship*, Vol. 31 (6), pp. 567-573.

Vezzosi, M. (2005). *Information Literacy and Reflective Learning: An Action Research Experience at the University of Pharma*. Newcastle: University of Northumbria.

Wallis, Jake (2005). Cyberspace, Information Literacy and the Information Society. *Library Review*, Vol. 54 (4), pp. 218-222.

Walsh, Andrew (2009). Information Literacy Assessment: Where Do We Start? *Journal of Librarianship and Information Science*, Vol. 41(1). pp. 19-28.

Wang, X. (2010). *Integrating Information Literacy into Higher Education Curriculum: An IL Curricular Integration Model*. Queensland University of Technology.

Webber, S. and Johnston, B. (2000). Conceptions of Information Literacy: New Perspectives and Implications. *Journal of Information Science*, Vol. 26(6), pp. 381-397.

Webber, S. and Johnston, B. (2002). Assessment for Information Literacy. *International Conference on IT and Information Literacy*. Glasgow, Scotland.

Welsh, Teresa S. and Wright, Mekissa S. (2010). Information Literacy in the Digital Age: An Evidence-Based Approach. Oxford: *Chandos Publishing*.

Wema, E. and Hepworth, M. (2007). An Evaluation of an Information Literacy Training Initiative at the University of Dares Salaam. *Journal of Information Literacy*, Vol. 1 (1), pp. 1-12.

Whitemore, E. (2001). A Longitudinal Study of Undergraduates' Academic Library Experiences. *Journal of Academic Librarianship*, Vol. 27 (5), pp. 379-385.

Whitemore, E. (2001). Development of Critical Thinking Skills: An Analysis of Academic Library Experiences and Other Measures. *College and Research Libraries*, Vol. 59 (3), pp. 266-273.

Willson, Rebekah (2012). Independent Searching During One-Shot Information Literacy Instruction Sessions: Is it an Effective Use of Time? *Evidence Based Library and Information Practice*, Vol. 7 (4), pp. 52-67.

Xiao, J. (2012). Integrating Information Literacy into Blackboard: Librarian-Faculty Collaboration for Successful Student Learning. *Library Management*, Vol. 31 (8/9), pp. 654-668.

Zhao, Jennifer Congyan and Mawhinney, Tara (2015). Comparison of Native Chinese-Speaking and Native English-Speaking Engineering Students' Information Literacy Challenges. *The Journal of Academic Librarianship*, Vol. 41. pp. 712-724.

Index

Q

R

❑ ❑ ❑